HOT DOGS

To My Canadian Girlfriend —
Just thought of you
and all the smiles
we would share reading it
Enjoy Karen!
Hugs Pam :)

HOT DOGS

SINGLE DOGS SEEKING SAME

NICHOLAS NOYES

Sterling Publishing, New York

A Sterling Book
Published by Sterling Publishing Co., Inc.
387 Park Avenue South, New York, NY 10016

©2005 by Sterling Publishing Co., Inc.

Distributed in Canada by Sterling Publishing
c/o Canadian Manda Group, 165 Dufferin Street
Toronto, Ontario M6K 3H6

Distributed in Great Britain by Chrysalis Books
64 Brewery Road, London N79NT, England
Distributed in Australia by Capricorn Link (Australia) Pty. Ltd.
P.O. Box 704, Windsor, NSW 2756, Australia

While this book may seem to encourage animal breeding, it is meant for entertainment purposes only.
Every day, tens of thousands of puppies and kittens are born, and every year tens of thousands of dogs and
cats cannot find a home and must be put to sleep as a result. In order to help diminish the overpopulation,
and consequent euthanasia of stray animals, please have your pet spayed or neutered. Thank you!

Photography Editor: Chris Bain
Additional photo research: Janice Ackerman, Lori Epstein
Digital Imaging: Daniel J. Rutkowski

ISBN 1-4027-3446-8

Library of Congress Cataloging-in-Publication Data

Noyes, Nicholas.
  Hot dogs : single dogs seeking same / Nicholas Noyes
    p. cm
Includes index.
ISBN 1-4027-3446-8
Dogs—Humor. 2. Personals—Humor. I. Title.
PN6231.D68N69 2005
818'.602—dc22
2005023663

Color separations by Friesens Corporation
Printed in Canada by Friesens Corporation
All rights reserved

10 9 8 7 6 5 4 3 2 1

Contents

Introduction

So you're a friendly, outgoing dog. You try to meet other canines wherever you go. Your grooming is fine, your human's no weirder than most, and you're good at putting out the "I'm available" vibes without seeming pushy. In other words, you're doing all you can to find that special dog and make a true Love Connection.

And yet, nothing seems to be working. The singles scene at the park is just too sleazy. And when you do meet a dog that you want to know better, it never seems to work out. The bitch you were ready to die for turns into a big bore when she's not in heat. . . your alpha-male dreamboat goes for your throat when you rib him for being so serious. . . a hissing Siamese transforms your sweet-nothing-whispering Romeo into a whimpering coward. . . .

Sound familiar? Well, Spot, you're not alone! Fortunately, you've come to the right place. Within the very pages you're drooling on right now are some of the most attractive eligible pooches to be found anywhere. Here, you'll meet dogs of every size, shape, color, and inclination. Each is a uniquely interesting individual, but they all share one thing in common: they're all looking to make a Love Connection, just like you!

The Categories

The personal ads in this volume are sorted into five broad categories, designed to make your love search as easy as possible.

Dams Seeking Sires

Gentlemen, start your engines! This chapter's packed chock-full of the loveliest lady-dogs in the land. You'll find good girls and bad girls, droolers and diggers, outdoor-adventure fanatics and lay-on-the-floor-all-day types. Are you the dog they're looking for? There's only one way to find out. . . .

Sires Seeking Dams

Calling all dams! Ladies, whether you're looking for a lascivious Lab, a jolly Jack Russell, a rabbit-killing Rottie, or a docile Dalmatian, you'll find him in here. Each hunky hound's looking for that one dam to share something special with—and there's no reason it can't be you!

Dams Seeking Dams

Whether you've always loved girls, you're naturally curious, or you're just plain sick of the company of single-minded male hump-freaks, you're bound to find a dam in this group that's looking for the same thing you are. In here, EVERY night is ladies' night.

Sires Seeking Sires

Boys, boys, boys! That's what we've got here—and they're all GOOD boys, if you know what I mean. . . . Take a look in here and get ready for a drool factor of 10! If you're a true dog's dog, this is where you'll want to look for that dominant Doberman or submissive St. Bernard you've been simply DYING to hook up with!

Anything Goes

Not looking for anything in the above categories? Maybe it's not romance you're after? Or perhaps your interests are a little, shall we say, unconventional? (Just doing it human-style now and then is certainly not YOUR idea of a wild sex life!) That's what this chapter's for. Whatever puts cheese in your Kibbles, there's a good chance it'll turn up here—and even if you don't find just what you're looking for, you may discover even more intriguing possibilities!

The Code System

Knowing that you don't want to spend all your time deciphering long lists of codes and letters, this book keeps it as simple as possible.

> **P** = **Purebred**
> **C** = **Crossbred**
>
> **A** = **Altered**
> **W** = **Whole**
>
> **S** = **Sire**
> **D** = **Dam**

For example, "PAS iso CWD" means "Purebred Altered Sire in search of Crossbred Whole Dam." But don't worry about deciphering these codes if you're in a hurry—they're just included as a general guideline to help you narrow your search.

Barking Up the Right Tree: Tips for Single Doggies on the Prowl

Once you've picked out a few ads that make you pant, or you've gotten some replies to your own ad, it will be time to take the next step: The First Date.

Whether you're hooking up for an afternoon romp in the park, prowling back alleys for delicacies, or lounging on the deck with a couple of friendly humans, there are a few key rules all romance-minded canines should observe. You may not make a Love Connection right away—but avoid these perpetual pet pitfalls and you can at least be sure you didn't chase Mr./Ms. Right away with a bad first impression!

Bad Dog!

Droolers—can we talk? You know who you are. I'm not talking about some yellow Lab who leaves a damp spot every time he sleeps over or some Setter who loves to lick too much. I'm talking to you Newfies and Rotties and Mastiffs, Bulldogs and Bassets and such—not all of you, just the ones with huge ropy gobs of semi-gelatinous slobber perpetually hanging down six inches from your oversize jowls.

Do humans often recoil from you in disgust? Do promising games of fetch peter out after a couple of tosses? Do other dogs near you always seem to be soaking wet? If so, I'm talking to you, and I've got three words: Wipe your face! Your date went to a lot of trouble choosing just the right scents for his/her coat. A quart of your slimy saliva will NOT be a welcome addition (unless they're into that kind of thing)—and it will definitely dampen your chances of making a Love Connection!

Bad Dog!

Got an "unusual" favorite goodie? Maybe you even get a bit...coprophagic at times? It's nothing to be embarrassed about, but remember: The first place your date's nose is going is your butt—and you'll have a better chance for romance if your more pungent preferences aren't the first thing he/she learns about you! So try to suppress those urges for at least 24 hours before your big date, ok?

Bad Dog!

Hey Killer! You play too rough! Whether you're a genuinely aggressive hothead who loses it at the drop of a tennis ball, or you just lose sight of the line between wrasslin' and fighting, you're making the dogs around you tense and uncomfortable.

Do we all secretly enjoy the sight of humans running around yelling their heads off? Of course! But there's a time and a place for everything—and that sort of behavior can quickly throw your Love Connection for a loop! A full belly helps some dogs keep things in check, while others say eating poppies (yummy!) and/or St John's Wort (not so yummy...) can make a big difference. Find what works for you, and turn your fight response down a few notches for date night, okay? Ya big brute!

Bad Dog!

Doggies, I hate to break it to you, but the plain fact is, your humans stink. Of course you don't notice! You're not only used to it, you're conditioned to like it. But just because you associate that special nose-bomb with comfort and a full belly—that particular mix of soap, shampoo, detergent, so-called deodorant, perfume, polyester, and whatever other poisons your human likes to roll in—that doesn't mean the same olfactory experience won't give your date a sudden headache (or worse!) that knocks the love train right off its rails.

Why take a chance? If you're bringing your human along for the big date, be sure to cover up any potentially offensive odors with a good smear of something both powerful and appetizing (horse dung is a sure-fire winner). And if you can arrange for your human to show up smelling like your pee, you won't just cover up the stink—you'll also make it mighty clear who holds the leash at your house!

Good Dog!
Be safe! Ladies—and fellas, too—you know that there are low-down curs out there who try to exploit this type of service and the honest, lonely hearts that benefit from it. Of course we strive to ensure that all the ads you find herein are on the level. But you can never be 100 percent sure, and it pays to be careful.

Tell your friends where you're going. Try to meet your date in a public place. If your human comes with you, be sure to keep it in sight at all times. And if your date yells "Hey, a rabbit!" and goes tearing off into the woods, remember that it could be true—but it could be a ruse to get you alone. Just try to use a little common sense, and trust your instincts.

So grab a nice big bone, settle onto your favorite rug, and dig in, dogs and dams! And when you find an ad that's got you licking the page, don't be shy. You never know— it just might be your Love Connection you're dragging your tongue across!

Happy Hunting!

DAMS
SEEKING
SIRES ♂
⚥

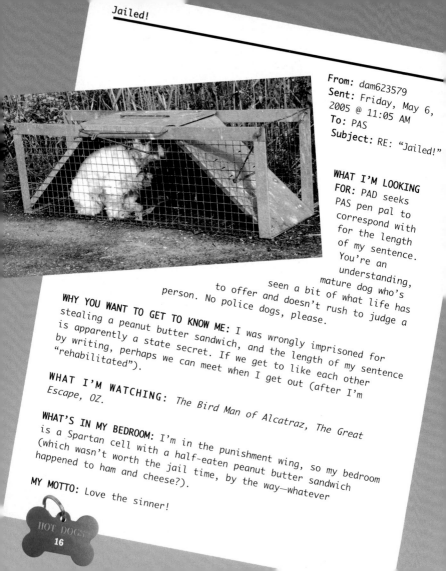

From: dam623579
Sent: Friday, May 6, 2005 @ 11:05 AM
To: PAS
Subject: RE: "Jailed!"

WHAT I'M LOOKING FOR: PAD seeks PAS pen pal to correspond with for the length of my sentence. You're an understanding, mature dog who's seen a bit of what life has to offer and doesn't rush to judge a person. No police dogs, please.

WHY YOU WANT TO GET TO KNOW ME: I was wrongly imprisoned for stealing a peanut butter sandwich, and the length of my sentence is apparently a state secret. If we get to like each other by writing, perhaps we can meet when I get out (after I'm "rehabilitated").

WHAT I'M WATCHING: The Bird Man of Alcatraz, The Great Escape, OZ.

WHAT'S IN MY BEDROOM: I'm in the punishment wing, so my bedroom is a Spartan cell with a half-eaten peanut butter sandwich (which wasn't worth the jail time, by the way—whatever happened to ham and cheese?).

MY MOTTO: Love the sinner!

COOL AND REFRESHING

WHAT I'M LOOKING FOR: Someone to help me get to the bottom of this bucket we call life. You're a sleek, large, dark, soft-spoken sire who's not afraid to lift me by the scruff of the neck and dunk me—repeatedly.

WHY YOU WANT TO GET TO KNOW ME: I'm dainty, a little fussy (but only about things that count), and I like to be pampered. I'm small, true, but very good with my tongue.

MY STRANGEST DREAM: I was drinking from a pool, when all of a sudden I realized that there were human children in the water—and we all know what kids do in the pool. Sure enough, I looked down and the water was completely yellow.

A SURPRISING FACT ABOUT ME: I used to only drink spring water as a puppy, but my owners got cheap and now I take what I can get.

MY MOTTO: Bottoms up!

HOT DOGS
17

Mama Bear

WHAT I'M LOOKING FOR: PWD seeks Papa Bear to make everything just right. You're a large PWS Labrador, who's into traditional Lab activities: crashing through underbrush, jumping into ponds, looking quizzically at humans as they try and guess what's on your mind (backatcha, ya big, bald monkeys!).

WHY YOU WANT TO GET TO KNOW ME: I'm a bit of a princess, living in high style with some pretty decent humans. Sometimes the strain of being responsible for all the Lab work in the house gets to me, and I feel I need a companion (and perhaps some puppies as well).

MY GREATEST AMBITION: To galumph through the Canadian Province that gives us our name.

WHAT'S IN MY BEDROOM: Four-poster bed, pink silk sheets, growing teddy bear collection (will you be the next one?).

MY MOTTO: Labs do it without thinking!

Call Tonight!

HOT DOGS

18

Basket Full of Fun

From: dam651
Sent: Sunday, June 22, 2005 @ 4:21 PM
To: CAS
Subject: RE: Basket Full of Fun

WHAT WE'RE LOOK-ING FOR: You're a striking Lab/Rottweiler sire with tubes tied, large shoulders, and slim hips. You better be all sire to be able to handle my sister and me!

WHY YOU WANT TO GET TO KNOW US: We're small PADs with big-dog appetites. If you think you're our pooch in shining armor, we'll wrap ourselves up in a bow and deliver ourselves to your door.

OUR FANTASY OWNER: Russell Crowe

PET PEEVES: Nothing spoils a romantic encounter so much as lack of follow-through. We expect our beaux to write thank-you notes, or at least give us a call after our dates.

OUR MOTTO: Two's company, three's the magic number.

HOT DOGS
19

Bling-Bling Baby

WHAT I'M LOOKING FOR: A lover who will shower me with gold collars, platinum dog-tags, and more—I'm worth it. You need to keep this girl in the style she's come to expect if you ever want to get your hump on.

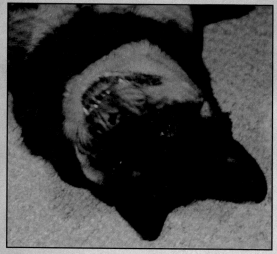

WHY YOU WANT TO GET TO KNOW ME: I like livin' large—from Versace collars to platinum 'n' ice tail rings—and you should, too. You: never settle for anything but the best. Me: the best.

MY FANTASY OWNER: Lil' Kim (but I ain't goin' to jail for nobody).

I'M MOST NEUROTIC ABOUT: Monies changin' the channel on me when I'm trying to watch Cribs. Look out—I'll bite yo ass!

MY MOTTO: If you don't shine, you ain't mine.

Masked Delight

What I'm Looking For: I'm in the midst of group therapy (which is the most committed relationship I've ever been in), but I'm taking baby steps back into the dating world after a messy breakup.
You: be a good listener, but don't pry behind the mask.

Why You Want To Get To Know Me: I'm like a locked kitchen cabinet packed with juicy bones: there's plenty to chew on here, once you get me to open up.

Favorite Thing To Do On A Date: Making faces, because I know he can't see what I'm doing.

My Hobbies Include: I collect masks from around the world. My favorite is a pink Venetian pig mask from Carnivale.

My Motto: If it's worth doing, it's worth doing in disguise.

HOT DOGS

21

WHAT I'M LOOKING FOR: You're a playful PWS who enjoys a noseful now and then.

WHY YOU WANT TO GET TO KNOW ME: I'm a hot young spaniel mix who likes to show off her best side. I'm mischievous and playful, but most of all I'm damn sexy. Baby got back, fellas!

MY PERFECT DATE: You're walking by and catch me digging in the dirt. You stop to admire my bod, then approach me slowly from behind. You take a long, slow breath—and it's love at first whiff.

WHAT'S IN MY BEDROOM: A nice, firm pillow that supports my stomach when I get worn out from constantly arching my back, conveniently located mirror (I like the view, too!).

MY MOTTO: The headquarters is in the hindquarters.

HOT DOGS
22

P E R S O N A L

DESPERATE HOUSEPETS DATING SERVICE

DAISY DUKE SEES BOSS DOG

WHAT I'M LOOKING FOR: I love all them country pastimes: huntin', fishin', backyard wrasslin', pumpkin chunking, and long, long walks. PWD looking for a C/PW sire who shares these interests, but has some of his own to bring to this here relationship thing.

WHY YOU WANT TO GET TO KNOW ME: I'm a rugged beauty, omnivorous, and one tough cookie. And all this here? It's my land.

MY PERFECT DATE: We have a mess of BBQ ribs, a coupl'a slurps of Jack, lie down, and leg-wrassle till the cows come home.

I'M MOST NEUROTIC ABOUT: What the hell does that mean?

MY MOTTO: Have ya ever seen a bumpkin chunk a punkin?

HOT DOGS

23

Big Mama Needs Some Lovin'

WHAT I'M LOOKING FOR: A sire who loves the large ladies, and knows how to make good use of my extra flesh. (Hint: it likes to be doused in drool.)

WHY YOU WANT TO GET TO KNOW ME: I've been told I'm cute and curvy, but what's most special about me is my big heart.

PET PEEVES: I hate it when my owners try to get me to exercise; I'm just not built that way. If I wanted to run after a ball, I would have been born a Retriever.

IF I WASN'T A DOG I'D LIKE TO BE: Ooooh, I think manatees are so cute!

MY MOTTO: The bigger the cushion, the sweeter the pushin'. . . .

Ooo La La!

HOT DOGS
24

Divorcée (I'm on the left)

WHAT I'M LOOKING FOR: Emerging from a bitter divorce, PAD is in search of kind, uncomplicated CAS (I don't think I could look at purebred right now, sorry), who's willing to help me with some healing.

WHY YOU WANT TO GET TO KNOW ME: The end of a relationship is complicated, not least because I shared a lot of my life, and even some happy memories, with the son-of-a-bitch. I am ready to try all those things they suggested in couples therapy with somebody who actually deserves my patience and respect.

I'M MOST NEUROTIC ABOUT: Well, to be honest, everything at this point.

MY PERFECT DATE: We can't go too near the dog run at the corner of North and Main—that's where I met him, and, can you believe it, he still hangs out there, the bastard!—but I would enjoy a walk in the park and maybe a quick piss on his lawn.

MY MOTTO: You can't take that away from me.

HOT DOGS

25

Let's Go Antiquing!

WHAT I'M LOOKING FOR: You're a PAS who is put together and adaptable. You're at home at a charity garbage auction and stripping a dumpster of edibles in a back alley. Bring your discerning taste.

WHY YOU WANT TO GET TO KNOW ME: My great joy is antiquing: I'm a PAD who likes nothing more than rooting about in a large pile of household refuse. There are some quite spectacular finds to be made.

WHAT I'M WATCHING: *This Old House, The Antiques Roadshow, Iron Chef.*

A SURPRISING FACT ABOUT ME: I slept on an old couch for weeks, not realizing that there was half a meatball sandwich under it (and I thought that couch just smelled good!).

MY MOTTO: One species' trash is another species' treasure.

What'll Ya Have?

What I'm Looking For: You're a sire who's sober, intelligent, buff, and funny. I'm asking a lot, so three out of four is fine (but no glue-sniffers, please). Most of all, you're sincere. I've got guys coming on to me all night, so what I don't need to hear is some cheesy pick-up line.

Why You Want To Get To Know Me: I work hard to satisfy my customers, and I've got quite a few tricks up my sleeve. I'm also very fashionable, as you can see.

Pet Peeves: Fighters, bores, long-winded guys, lousy tippers. Oh, and I can out-party you, so don't even try.

What I'm Watching: *Trees Lounge*, *Cheers* reruns, *Cocktail*. I've never seen *Coyote Ugly* and wouldn't mind keeping it that way.

My Motto: Pay up, bub.

Rascally Rabbits

From: dam365
Sent: Wednesday, May 11, 2005 @ 4:57 PM
To: C/PWS
Subject: RE: Rascally Rabbits

WHAT I'M LOOKING FOR: A firm disciplinarian to help me keep these bad little toys in line. You're a patient and fair C/PW sire, but know that toys need discipline. We'll round them up, bark at them, then drag them all over the house until they're bedraggled tangles of fur and slobber.

WHY YOU WANT TO GET TO KNOW ME: I may seem a little single-minded in my devotion to my "house pets," but in reality this PAD has a wide range of interests, including what the neighbors' cat is doing (that little hussy), and growling at strange shoes.

WHAT I'M BEGGING FOR: A little liverwurst on a pretzel.

WHAT'S IN MY BEDROOM: A bed, under which you will find the fluffy remains of naughty toys.

MY MOTTO: Constant vigilance is the price of freedom.

IS THE DOCTOR IN?

WHAT I'M LOOKING FOR: I'm in a rut and need an antidote to the tedium. You're a CAS with the patience to see my good points while (sorry!) dealing with some of the emotional baggage I'll bring to our relationship.

WHY YOU WANT TO GET TO KNOW ME: On my good days I'm a playful, sexy, and fit CAD, but on some days I just want stay in bed and pull the covers over my head. Either way, your bedside manner comes in handy!

PET PEEVES: Self-help books and preachy humans—what do they know about a dog's life?

MY GREATEST AMBITION: To see the water bowl as half full, for once.

MY MOTTO: Tomorrow is another day.

HOT DOGS
29

The Dog**s** **Gazette**

It's the Age of Aquarius

WHAT I'M LOOKING FOR: PAD seeks P/CW/AS soul mate who understands astrology and is comfortable visiting my psychic (an Old English Sheepdog) for relationship advice. No Scorpios (sorry, it just wouldn't work).

WHY YOU WANT TO GET TO KNOW ME: I'm a classic water dog: creative, open to new experiences, and eager to get all wet. Let's splash our way through life.

WHAT I'M WATCHING: *Hair, Woodstock, Snoopy Come Home.*

PET PEEVES: Dog groomers, uptight German Shepherds, leash laws, Dionne Warwick (Psychic Hotline my ass!).

MY MOTTO: You've got to be up to see the dawn.

Dig This!

From: dam8891
Sent: Saturday, June 25, 2005 @ 10:15 AM
To: CWS
Subject: RE: Dig This!

WHAT I'M LOOKING FOR: A CW sire who has a LOT of stuff—bones, toys, etc.—and a taste for hide-and-seek. If I'm not digging and burying I don't know what to do with myself.

WHY YOU WANT TO GET TO KNOW ME: If you've been good, I'll bury your reward for later; if you've been bad, I'll bury the evidence; and if you're into it, I'll bury you.

I'M MOST NEUROTIC ABOUT: Don't come near my dig sites unless I tell ya it's okay—that's how dogs get hurt.

IF I WASN'T A DOG I'D LIKE TO BE: A ferret. They eat prairie dogs (which are not real dogs) and take over their burrows.

MY MOTTO: It's down there, somewhere!

HOT DOGS!

Confident Pug

WHAT I'M LOOKING FOR: You're a pug who's secure in your identity as a small dog: you're relaxed, mellow, and not afraid to hump a leg. Self-confidence is sexy—PWS only, please!

WHY YOU WANT TO GET TO KNOW ME: This hot little PAD will lick just about anything....

MOST EMBARRASSING MOMENT: I once licked the black right off another pug's nose! How was I to know the guy was a crossbred poseur wearing makeup?

MY PERFECT DAY: I take a stroll and test my tongue on new surfaces. Some good ones I've found recently are iron furniture, rubber tires, and the insides of toilet bowls, though that last one can be tricky without falling in.

MY MOTTO: Give a licking and keep on ticking.

Hotcha!

A Bad Habit

What I'm Looking For:
A Saint Bernard with all his parts intact to show this wayward soul the light, or at least a good time. Judgment day will soon be upon us, so let's live it up and put our God-given bodies to good use.

Why You Want To Get To Know Me: You know what they say about Catholic girls? That's just the half of it....

My Hobbies Include:
Drinking holy water from the baptismal font, sneaking hosts, and chewing up rosaries (hail Mary this, all you holy rollers!).

What's In My Bedroom:
The other half of this scratchy habit that my masters make me wear on Sundays (can you tell this is one sister who isn't cut out for the convent?).

My Motto: Confess to me.

From: dam394
Sent: Sunday, June 12, 2005 @ 1:40 PM
To: PWD
Subject: RE: Calling the Booty Monster

WHAT I'M LOOKING FOR: I already have a best friend (he feeds me, pets me, and takes me for walks): I need a lover. You're a well-built PWS who's all that and a bag of rawhide chips. You better eat right, because you're going to need stamina to keep up with this speedy little PWD.

WHY YOU WANT TO GET TO KNOW ME: As tireless as I am inventive, I will make sure you won't find our time together boring. I'm tired of puppies who sniff and sniff and never get down. Are you up for the challenge?

WHAT I'M LISTENING TO: Pink's "Get This Party Started" and Eve's "Dog Match."

WHAT'S IN MY BEDROOM: Queen-size dog bed with silk sheets, a black velvet canopy, and a collection of aromatherapy candles.

MY MOTTO: I'll roll over for you.

CANDY GIRL

WHAT I'M LOOKING FOR: You're a big PW sire (big compared to me, that is—maybe a Scottish Terrier or a Corgi) with a sweet tooth. You're practically perfect in every way, just like me; together we'll be cute as peaches!

WHY YOU WANT TO GET TO KNOW ME: Let me be your candy and in return I'll lick your lollipop all night long.

A SURPRISING FACT ABOUT ME: My first human was a dentist, so I've got nice teeth and sweet breath!

WHAT I'M WATCHING: *The Wizard of Oz, Willy Wonka and the Chocolate Factory.*

MY MOTTO: Hard candy shell, soft center.

Overrun!

WHAT I'M LOOKING FOR: I need a sire who loves pups—and lots of 'em!—to help me baby-sit my brood. It doesn't take much to look after them, I promise—they don't really move around too much on their own!—and I'll make it worth your while.

WHY YOU WANT TO GET TO KNOW ME: If I can handle all this, I can handle anything. I'm responsible, clearly, and have done well for myself, though the future financial strain of supporting this many puppies might prove overwhelming on my own. Think of me as a DILF!

A SECRET MOST OTHERS DON'T KNOW ABOUT ME: I never wanted kids! I don't know how all this happened. They just appeared in my room one day.

WHAT'S IN MY BEDROOM: Twenty pairs of shoebox-cribs and a box of Lincoln Logs for when they start teething.

MY MOTTO: One dollar and a teat short....

Sexy Mama!

Princess Needs Prince

From: dam623579
Sent: Tuesday, April 26, 2005 @ 11:05 AM
To: PWS
Subject: Princess Needs Prince

WHAT I'M LOOKING FOR: PWS with good manners and a noble air. You'll treat me like royalty, and ensure that the flashbulbs don't get too close, this picture notwithstanding. Finicky eaters fine (preferable, even).

WHY YOU WANT TO GET TO KNOW ME: I'm a petite redhead, and just a little shy. After my last relationship ended it felt like a dynasty had crumbled. I'm ready to get my feet wet again (that's a metaphor—I absolutely HATE to get my feet wet), and welcome worthy suitors.

WHAT'S IN MY BEDROOM: The very softest of dog beds, a lavender pillow, bottles of Magie Noire.

MY STRANGEST DREAM: I dreamt I was a common mutt, mindlessly retrieving a rotten tennis ball for my master. How horrid!

MY MOTTO: The world is my oyster.

HOT DOGS
37

Tiny Little Dish

WHAT I'M LOOKING FOR: PAD seeks kind, mature PAS to look after her. You're considerate, patient, and you never, ever snap at dinnertime.

WHY YOU WANT TO GET TO KNOW ME: I'm small and alone in the big city. I find dog runs scary (the little dogs gossip about you, the big dogs knock you over, the terriers are always freaking out), and the hydrant scene is too anonymous for real relationships.

A SECRET MOST OTHERS DON'T KNOW ABOUT ME: When I was a baby I slept in a shoe.

MY PERFECT DATE: My favorite thing to do is to go sniffing around in a large house, so a date at a museum or historical site would be perfect. I'm a dog who likes her creature comforts, so a nice meal would be appreciated, too, followed by some quality time on a comfortable *chaise longue*.

MY MOTTO: Sunday's dog is full of grace.

Busy Bee

What I'm Looking For: A hardworking PAS who understands the demands of a busy, upwardly mobile PAD. I don't have much time for you, but the time we do have, boy, better be good!

Why You Want To Get To Know Me: I work hard, I play hard. I've never run up a bill that I couldn't make disappear with a scratch of my paw, and, as you can see, I have my own private chauffeur.

What I'm Watching: Wall Street, In the Company of Men, American Psycho.

What's In My Bedroom: Motivational posters, a BlackBerry dock, and a paper shredder—though I prefer to shred important documents orally.

My Motto: All work and no play makes Jill a dull girl.

From: dam22
Sent: Monday, May 16, 2005 @ 5:30 AM
To: CWS
Subject: RE: Multicultural Holiday

WHAT I'M LOOKING FOR: Like me, you're from a family with blended traditions (Note to mom: blended tradition does not mean a matzo-ball smoothie), who's at home in two (or more) cultures.

WHY YOU WANT TO GET TO KNOW ME: I'm a CWD whose upbringing makes me sensitive to other dogs' backgrounds. Let's swim in the melting pot together and make some crossbred, interfaith pups of our own.

MY FAVORITE HOLIDAY: Every year I swear it's too much, and that next December I'm just going to go hang out on a Caribbean beach somewhere, but every year I end up celebrating both Christmas and Hanukkah, trees and menorahs, side by side.

WORST LIE I EVER TOLD: Told mom that the matzo-ball smoothie "wasn't that bad."

MY MOTTO: I'll try any tradition at least once.

HOT DOGS
40

TIE ME UP, TIE ME DOWN

WHAT I'M LOOKING FOR: PWD seeks adventuresome companion for role playing/light bondage. You are an open-minded, dominant but gentle PWS unafraid of the opportunities life has to offer. Familiarity with the Klingon language a BIG plus.

WHY YOU WANT TO GET TO KNOW ME: I'll let you be my master. And let me tell you, I know how to serve.

WHAT I'M LISTENING TO: Marilyn Manson's *Holy Wood (In the Valley of the Shadow of Death)*, Gary Numan's *The Pleasure Principle*.

WHAT'S IN MY BEDROOM: Complete set of unchewed first edition posable action figures from the first *Star Wars* trilogy and assorted "love toys," including PVC bondage swing built to accommodate four-legged playmates.

MY MOTTO: Wear sunglasses if you've got bags under your eyes.

HOT DOGS

41

Let Me Be Your Trophy Babe

WHAT I'M LOOKING FOR: Poolside beauty seeks country-club PWS with good manners and excellent taste.

WHY YOU WANT TO GET TO KNOW ME: I'm an expert sunbather and lounger, and I'm always happy to look after your stuff while you use the bathroom.

THINGS I LIKE TO PICK UP AND HIDE: Suntan lotion, tennis bracelets, sunglasses.

WHAT'S IN MY BEDROOM: A collection of collars in lime green, pink, and red, with navy-blue whales, a monogrammed dog bed, and a framed print of *Miss Anna Ward with Her Dog*, by Sir Joshua Reynolds.

MY MOTTO: You take care of everything else and I'll take care of you.

Smiling all the Time

From: dam1001
Sent: Friday, May 27, 2005 @ 1:25 AM
To: PAS
Subject: RE: Smiling all the Time

WHAT I'M LOOKING FOR: Do you make a wish when you see a painted hydrant? Do you sometimes howl at the sun? Are you an eccentric poet, a beachcomber, gypsy, or bum? Then we need to meet!

WHY YOU WANT TO GET TO KNOW ME: I got tired of dogs who live bankers' hours. I'm a reformed little doggy, finally enjoying life, who wants to love a little before she gets too old. I'm an inquisitive, alert PAD with a nose colder than an Alaskan milkshake. Let's poke around town a little and see what turns up.

WORST LIE I EVER TOLD: "We can work things out."

MY PERFECT DATE: We collaborate on digging an interesting and artistic hole, turn over a few garbage cans, and sneak through a couple of back alleys before arriving at the park after dark, where we play checkers in the moonlight.

MY MOTTO: Over the hill, but gaining momentum.

Love Me, Love My Humans!

WHAT I'M LOOKING FOR: A human-enthusiast to meet for walks in the park. Let's see if our people get along, and take it from there.

WHY YOU WANT TO GET TO KNOW ME: When I'm not talking about my pets, I'm a good conversationalist and eager listener. Other pastimes include eating out, hiking, and collecting people dolls.

ABOUT MY PETS: My humans are lively, highly intelligent (I swear they have their own favorite TV programs, and try and look around me if I get in the way!), and—get this—think they own the place! I have to continuously chase them off the furniture.

WHAT'S IN MY BEDROOM: Cute pictures of my people, human hair (the male sheds a lot, but oddly enough his hair doesn't grow back).

MY MOTTO: It's like they understand everything I say.

Call Tonight!

HOT DOGS

44

The Cats' Meow

What I'm Looking For: You don't have to love cats, or even like them especially much, but you don't regard them as prey. Still, if you value cats for what they are—smallish animals that desperately wish they were dogs—you are the sort of open-minded PAS I'm looking for.

Why You Want To Get To Know Me: I wanted puppies of my own but the butcher (that's the vet to you) tied my tubes, so I had to settle for the next best thing—I'm a hardworking foster mom raising a litter of kittens. Still, I can't spend all day chasing around after the kits—I'm saving all my dog love for the right sire.

Worst Lie I Ever Told: "Don't worry honey, cats are just as good as dogs."

What's In My Bedroom: A litter box, hairballs, and yarn. And a Mastiff-sized "magic wand" (which I'd get rid of, if you insisted).

My Motto: Relax, cats don't know any better.

Like a Rolling Stone

WHAT I'M LOOKING FOR:
A back-up howler, and if you can play the bongos, even better. Must enjoy the street life; pampered house pets need not apply.

WHY YOU WANT TO GET TO KNOW ME: I'm a talented singer-songwriter who enjoys howling on subways and outside Starbucks (people always give me the change from their café lattes). I'm street smart and can survive on my own, but I wouldn't mind sharing my hard-won earnings with the right sire.

WHAT I'M LISTENING TO: Ani DiFranco, Jewel, Bob Dylan, and Murphy, the dog in the dumpster next door.

MY GREATEST AMBITION: To play a sold-out show in the alley outside Madison Square Garden.

MY MOTTO: Sing it, sister!

ELLE OF THE BALL

WHAT I'M LOOKING FOR: Clean-cut, gallant PAS from hunting or herding breed, with an old-world chivalric sensibility. Let's meet for iced tea sometime and get to know each other.

WHY YOU WANT TO GET TO KNOW ME: I'm a beautiful, petite Southern dam who appreciates the finer things in life: chintz window treatments, potpourri, divinity, pink lemonade, and lavender talc.

WHAT I'M READING: *Wuthering Heights, Ivanhoe, Gone with the Wind.*

WORST LIE I EVER TOLD: "Why, you certainly do know how to make a mint julep."

MY MOTTO: Good girls don't pant.

HOT DOGS

47

Always the Bridesmaid

WHAT I'M LOOKING FOR: An older, gentlemanly PAS, preferably with some legal background. Someone who is looking to be in it for the long haul—marriage, puppies, and beyond.

WHY YOU WANT TO GET TO KNOW ME: I was disappointed in love several years ago by my fiancé, who jilted me at the altar. He never returned, though I kept the wedding feast exactly as he left it for six months afterward! Which is an excellent example of my famed attention to detail.

MY HOBBIES INCLUDE: Attempting to preserve deviled eggs. They actually stay tasty for as long as 2 years, although the taste really only develops after the first couple of months.

WHAT'S IN MY BEDROOM: My bridal dress, which I try on occasionally (see picture).

MY MOTTO: Fool me once, shame on you....

Ooo La La!

From: dam2242
Sent: Friday, May 20, 2005 @ 6:55 AM
To: C/PAS
Subject: RE: Batteries Not Included

WHAT I'M LOOKING FOR: Playtime didn't end on your 1st birthday, and won't on your 8th. We're a frisky species, and playing adult games keeps us young and healthy. If you wish to experiment with introducing toys and elements of play into your erotic life, we should get together.

WHY YOU WANT TO GET TO KNOW ME: I love big toys.

MY FAVORITE TOYS: The belly-scratcher, *Mr. Magic Spot*, *Stiffy*, and *Behind the Ears!*

I'M MOST NEUROTIC ABOUT: Bad, messy dogs who don't put toys away after they've finished with them.

MY MOTTO: Play with me (but only if you mean it!).

HOT DOGS
49

A Taxing Woman

WHAT I'M LOOKING FOR: I want to help you with your taxes, go out for coffee and donuts, and, who knows, perhaps romance will bloom by the numbers!

WHY YOU WANT TO GET TO KNOW ME: With my accountant's training we'll keep track of all our assets: chew toys, bones, tasty meat nuggets, and doggy smooches.

MY FAVORITE HOLIDAY: April 15th: I like to go down to the post office and bark at the disorganized fools who are filing at the last minute.

MY FAVORITE PIECE OF FURNITURE: The file-cabinet drawer where mother kept us as puppies.

MY MOTTO: Cheaters never prosper.

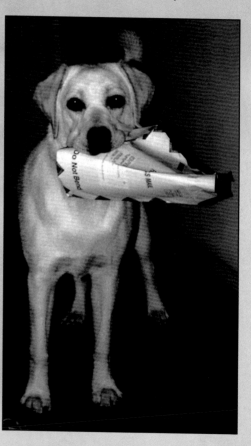

Don't Believe in Love?

What I'm Looking For: Canine cynic open to giving love one last chance. You're a CAS who's been bruised and battered by the tumble dryer of love, but it hasn't quite killed the romantic in you. Let's dance for Cupid one more time.

Why You Want To Get To Know Me: Like you, I've been through dating hell, but I cling to the idea that there is a good relationship for me somewhere, with someone. Other people have them—why not us?

What I'm Watching: You've Got Mail, Sleepless in Seattle, Annie Hall, the mailbox (for a letter from you!).

My Perfect Date: One that doesn't end in a flea bath.

My Motto: Maybe this won't suck.

HOT DOGS

51

Punk-Rock Queen

WHAT I'M LOOKING FOR: A slamming, skunking, moshing, pogoing dog of few words, but with lots and lots of energy.

WHY YOU WANT TO GET TO KNOW ME: I'm a free spirit who finds a creative outlet in the out-of-control mayhem of the mosh pit, and in listening to music at decibels equivalent to a jumbo jet making an emergency landing during a hurricane.

WHAT I'M LISTENING TO: Bow Wow Wow, Rancid, KMFDM, Rammstein.

MY FAVORITE TOYS: Spark plug from a '57 Ford, left leg of Joey Ramone's favorite jeans, discarded jumbo safety pin.

MY MOTTO: Hey! HO! Let's GO!

P E R S O N A L S

THE MOST WONDERFUL TIME OF THE YEAR

WHAT I'M LOOKING FOR: CWD seeks CAS with a sense of wonder, for whom each day is as exciting and special as Christmas (even if it's largely due to chronic memory loss).

WHY YOU WANT TO GET TO KNOW ME: We can have Christmas every day of the (human) year. Each morning, before dawn, we'll share the excitement of opening a surprise gift, followed by a robust session of Yuletide lovemaking.

WHAT I'M WATCHING: *Miracle on 34th Street, It's a Wonderful Life, White Christmas.*

MY PERFECT DATE: After hanging our stockings with care, we take a long winter's nap; when we wake up, it's Christmas. Time to get unwrapped, baby!

MY MOTTO: That's ME on top of the tree!

HOT DOG

53

Waiting for Our Sire

WHAT WE'RE LOOKING FOR: This playful pair of CAD sisters is just panting at the door for our sires to come. You're two large breeds with boundless energy and sunny dispositions who can handle an eager pair.

WHY YOU WANT TO GET TO KNOW US: Without a sire around, we've resorted to bickering with each other (much as humans do). But with a couple of big dogs to adore and obey, we'll get along like puppies.

WHAT'S IN OUR BEDROOM: A 40" round L.L. Bean bed that fits both of us with room to spare; our collection of matching designer outfits.

OUR PERFECT DAY: We're sitting together, staring out at the yard, when suddenly you both appear, galloping toward us, your tongues flapping in the wind, barking and leaping with anticipation.

OUR MOTTO: Big things come in big packages.

Call Tonight!

HOT DOGS
54

The Good Life, at Last

From: dam623
Sent: Tuesday, June 7, 2005 @ 10:17 AM
To: PAS
Subject: RE: The Good Life, at Last

WHAT I'M LOOKING FOR: Mature altered Airedale dam seeks PAS for leisurely weekends antiquing in the country, dinner parties filled with laughter and barking, and early morning strolls on the beach. You're healthy, but well past your puppy exuberance. No midlife crises, please.

WHY YOU WANT TO GET TO KNOW ME: I'm a kind and loving soul, though I can appear aloof. I'm financially secure and have nearly everything I need, except for that special dog to share it with. I love to travel, but I'm through with roughing it; no cargo cabins or third-rate kennels when we hit the road.

WHAT'S IN MY JOURNAL: I like to note the change in seasons— little things like buds appearing in the trees, the first snowdrop of spring, or a new scent on the local hydrant.

WHAT I'M READING: *Dogs Who Run with the Women Who Run with the Wolves*, *No Bad Dogs: The Woodhouse Way*, *Mrs. Dalloway*.

MY MOTTO: Older and bolder.

Cooling My Heels

WHAT I'M LOOKING FOR: Hey, old timer! Maybe we can teach other some new tricks! I'm looking for a seasoned PAS who can still tell the difference between himself and his dog bed.

WHY YOU WANT TO GET TO KNOW ME: Country PWD, gentle, loves all things aquatic, nearly 9 (but people don't believe I'm a great-grandmother—39 times!). Let's chase some ducks together and see where that leads us.

MY FAVORITE PHYSICAL ACTIVITY: Tearing away from my human's side and taking a running leap into a weed-filled duck pond. The combination of adrenaline rush and amusement at my humans crying pathetically at the dismal prospect of a wet dog in the car is an unbelievable high.

WHAT'S IN MY BEDROOM: Ducks Unlimited wooden dog bed, four South Carolinian hand-carved duck decoys, a warm eiderdown comforter, a framed Audubon print.

MY MOTTO: When in doubt, DUCK!

READY FOR MY CLOSE-UP

WHAT I'M LOOKING FOR: Paid gentleman companion. I need your experience and help running a large household, as well as with a few chores of a personal nature. Attention to ME a must.

WHY YOU WANT TO GET TO KNOW ME: I'm a talented and well-known PAD thespian. I've retired from acting (I was "Teenybelle" for five seasons on *One World to Turn*), but I'm still very much at the top of my game, and will return for that special project. I still have much to give to the profession.

WHAT I'M WATCHING: *Sunset Boulevard, Mommie Dearest, Whatever Happened to Baby Jane?*

WHAT'S IN MY CLOSET: Wooden hangers and lots of couture. A skeleton or two....

MY MOTTO: It's the pictures that got small.

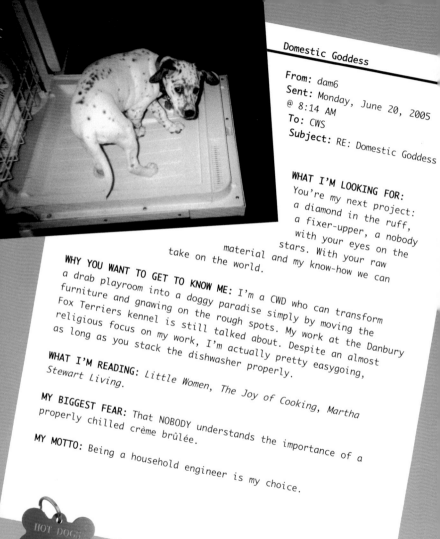

Domestic Goddess

From: dam6
Sent: Monday, June 20, 2005 @ 8:14 AM
To: CWS
Subject: RE: Domestic Goddess

WHAT I'M LOOKING FOR: You're my next project: a diamond in the ruff, a fixer-upper, a nobody with your eyes on the stars. With your raw material and my know-how we can take on the world.

WHY YOU WANT TO GET TO KNOW ME: I'm a CWD who can transform a drab playroom into a doggy paradise simply by moving the furniture and gnawing on the rough spots. My work at the Danbury Fox Terriers kennel is still talked about. Despite an almost religious focus on my work, I'm actually pretty easygoing, as long as you stack the dishwasher properly.

WHAT I'M READING: Little Women, The Joy of Cooking, Martha Stewart Living.

MY BIGGEST FEAR: That NOBODY understands the importance of a properly chilled crème brûlée.

MY MOTTO: Being a household engineer is my choice.

HOT DOGS
58

Malibu Marvel

What I'm Looking For: I'm tired of Frisbee dogs with bandannas and short-term memory loss. You're a beachcombing PWS with an interest in real estate and a strong territorial instinct. Surfing skills a big plus.

Why You Want To Get To Know Me: This beach babe enjoys quiet days by the pool and partying hard at night. With my knowledge of the good life, I'm one PWD who knows how to treat you right.

What I'm Listening To: The Beach Boys, Steely Dan, The Eagles, Jimmy Buffett.

My Perfect Day: A poolside breakfast of fresh fruit and raw meat, followed by some sunbathing, a light lunch, and an afternoon menacing human surfers with you.

My Motto: Life's a bitch (and a damn good one, too!).

Rescue Us!

WHAT WE'RE LOOKING FOR: We need a daring CAS to plan and execute our rescue, and to whisk us away to paradise. You'll have to be cunning, brave, and good with your teeth to free us from our captor's clutches. And once we're liberated, your stamina will come in handy....

WHY YOU WANT TO GET TO KNOW US: Being held captive for so long, we've become very, very horny. Sure, we can take care of ourselves, but it's just not the same.

WHAT WE'D BE WATCHING IF WE HAD A TV IN OUR CELL: *The Great Escape*, *The Shawshank Redemption*, *Escape from New York*.

MOST EMBARASSING MOMENT: Every second we're out in public like this is an embarassment. Even the dogs that walk by on leashes stick their tongues out at us.

OUR MOTTO: Freedom now!

Hotcha!

HOT DOGS

60

Mardi Gras Babe

From: dam333
Sent: Wednesday, April 13, 2005 @ 5:34 PM
To: CWS
Subject: RE: Mardi Gras Babe

WWHAT I'M LOOKING FOR: Hot-blooded PWD seeks CWS who'll shower me in beads and make sure I get the piece of cake with the baby in it.

WHY YOU WANT TO GET TO KNOW ME: You don't get Mardi Gras beads by being a good girl—in the Big Easy you're either big, easy, or both!

MY FAVORITE PHYSICAL ACTIVITY: Baring my nipples and pleasuring you all night long.

MY THREE FAVORITE COCKTAILS: The Sazerac, the Hurricane, and the Absinthe Frappe.

MY MOTTO: "Laissez les bon temps roulez."

From: dam135
Sent: Saturday, June 11 2005 @ 8:41 PM
To: PAS
Subject: RE: Ten Points for Gryffindor!

WWHAT I'M LOOKING FOR: Mid-level-to-advanced wizard with established transformational abilities (let's make bones!). Own cap and hat essential. Let's get together to see if the magic is there. No muggles, please.

WHY YOU WANT TO GET TO KNOW ME: I play well with others, but do not hesitate to stand up for myself. An avowed enemy of You-Know-Who, I nonetheless know how to have a good time. Plus, I'm a Corgi. What's not to like?

WHAT I'M READING: Harry Potter and the Half-Blood Prince, The Lord of the Rings trilogy, The Chronicles of Earthsea, and The Dark Is Rising.

WHAT'S IN MY BEDROOM: A vast collection of slightly chewed-up wands, brooms, and wizarding staffs. Dungeons and Dragons commemorative figurines.

MY MOTTO: "Do not meddle in the affairs of wizards, for they are subtle and quick to anger."

HOT DOGS
62

LOOKING FOR DOGTOR LIVINGSTONE

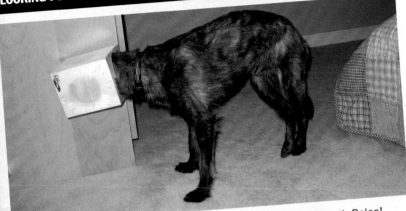

WHAT I'M LOOKING FOR: Dogs helped discover the North and South Poles! Dogs were the first to explore space! Nonetheless, love remains a jungle to this searcher, so I need an intrepid CAS with a flawless sense of direction to help me find my way to happiness.

WHY YOU WANT TO GET TO KNOW ME: I'm a curious and youthful CAD with a keen appreciation of the ridiculous. I come from a long line of showdogs (on my dad's side), but I'm quite modest by nature (I promise I won't wear the box when we date!).

PET PEEVES: Dogs who say I have a fat head—I'm just big-cheekboned.

WHAT'S IN MY BEDROOM: This is embarrassing, but I frequently have a hard time finding my bedroom. As a result, I often sleep on the couch. It's a nice couch.

MY MOTTO: Love: the dark continent!

Cantankerous Crank

WHAT I'M LOOKING FOR: PAD seeks companion with whom to attend the 5th reunion of my dog-training class. Tired of all those condescending looks and pity-filled sniffs when you show up solo at social events? Fed up with being the bitter one nursing a chew toy in the corner alone? I feel ya. Let's weave a fantasy so rich that those other mongrels will feel like crap for a change.

WHY YOU WANT TO GET TO KNOW ME: I've got a biting wit and I take no shit.

IF I WASN'T A DOG I'D LIKE TO BE: A grizzly. As adults, grizzly bears are solitary except during their brief, but earthshaking, mating season.

WORST LIE I EVER TOLD (REPEATEDLY): "Pictures of your children? How fascinating!"

MY MOTTO: If you don't have anything nice to say, come sit next to me.

Sophisticate / Aristocrat

What I'm Looking For: Intellectually vivacious and financially rotund PAS who will support my every artistic endeavor.

Why You Want To Get To Know Me: Supporting my art will make your life more meaningful, and reporters are just dying to cover the next high-power society couple—that could be us!

What I'm Reading: *The History of Sexuality*, by Michel Foucault, *ArtNews*.

What's In My Bedroom: An easel, a darkroom, a writing desk, a film studio, a recording studio. . . it's a lot to keep up with, I know, but my talent simply can't be contained.

My Motto: Art frees the soul—money frees the art.

It's Easy Being Me!

WHAT I'M LOOKING FOR: CWD seeks patient, understanding PAS who's used to working with small children or the insane. No egomaniacs—one's enough, trust me!

WHY YOU WANT TO GET TO KNOW ME: I'm terrific—no, really! When I lie here like this (see picture), nobody can resist me. They touch me, they rub me, they coo under their breath. What other proof do I need to know I'm the bee's knees?

WHAT I'M READING: *How to Win Friends and Influence People*, by Dale Carnegie, *A Different Kind of Intimacy: The Collected Writings of Karen Finley*.

WHAT'S IN MY BEDROOM: A large picture window with no curtains, a full-length mirror, and lots of photos of a really sexy little dog I know....

MY MOTTO: All me, all the time (oh, yeah, and you, too, a little bit).

Sexy Mama!

I'll Eat You Up, I Love You So

From: dam958
Sent: Tuesday, June 28, 2005 @ 6:11 PM
To: P/CAS
Subject: RE: I'll Eat You Up, I Love You So

WHAT I'M LOOKING FOR:
My ice cream man: a P/CAS who's sweet, soft (maybe even a little plump!), and happy to be licked from the top of his scoop to the bottom of his cone.

WHY YOU WANT TO GET TO KNOW ME: I'm a PAD with a sweet tooth, and I'm always hungry for more. I'm a connoisseur of fine foods looking for the perfect main course—could you be on the menu?

MY PERFECT DAY: It's August, the so-called dog days of summer. It's so hot the streets are sticky, and my pads are getting a little fried. Suddenly, a human child drops his ice-cream cone on the ground. As he cries like a puppy, you and I eat it right then and there as it melts on the sidewalk. Our tongues touch....

WHAT I'M BEGGING FOR: Crème brulee, but I'd settle for flan in a pinch.

MY MOTTO: *Chacun à son goût.*

HOT DOGS
67

Romantic in Winter

WHAT I'M LOOKING FOR: PAD looking for a darkly handsome PAS to sweep me off my feet. We don't have to get on at first; in fact, if I initially think you're an arrogant cad and you find me to be a flibberty gibbet upon meeting, so much the better.

WHY YOU WANT TO GET TO KNOW ME: I'm a published author of the Regency Romance series *Lord Beagle of Cleavedom Park* and *The Hounds of Dashitt Hall*. My fierce pride, ultimately, will be an asset to our relationship.

MY HOBBIES INCLUDE: Floral decorating, historical reenactment, and motorized jousting on skidoos.

WHAT YOU'LL FIND IN MY DIARY: Appointments with my hairdresser, meetings with my agent, and the phone number of the cute, younger Dalmatian I met at the coffee shop.

MY MOTTO: "It is a truth universally acknowledged that a dog in possession of bones must be in want of a bite."

EARTH MOTHER

WHAT I'M LOOKING FOR: PAD seeks sire, all breeds considered, altered or whole. You're a kind and loving companion who will join me in (nonviolently) guarding the good earth. I know every dog wants a little meat now and then, but willingness to try vegetarianism a plus.

WHY YOU WANT TO GET TO KNOW ME: I'm a healthy, outdoorsy Democrat who recycles, is opposed to oil drilling, and mistrusts politicians (especially from Texas).

WHAT I EAT: I've been a raw vegan for two years, and apart from the terrible gas that results, I've never felt healthier.

WHAT I'M LISTENING TO: Grateful Dead bootlegs (I followed them with my human for 2 years), Neil Young, Joni Mitchell, Phish, and Willie Nelson.

MY MOTTO: It's my nature to nurture.

HOT DOG

69

I Need a Dog Who Can Bring Relief

WHAT I'M LOOKING FOR: Older PWD seeks younger dog. You're a small-to-mid-size dog in the 1 to 3 (tops!) range, in good shape, and frisky but not foolish. Must have all shots. Sorry, no mutts and no nuts!

WHY YOU WANT TO GET TO KNOW ME: Experience is a great teacher, and believe me, I'm experienced. After my last divorce left me in the position of never needing another sugar doggy, I retired to my beach condo and the pursuit of life's pleasures.

WHAT I'M WATCHING: The Graduate, Summer of '42, Bull Durham, The Westminster Dog Show (was that you I saw acing the agility course?).

MY FAVORITE PHYSICAL ACTIVITIES: Walks on the beach, obviously, but I'm also a keen swimmer. I really like to keep in shape for my favorite physical activity, which I'll gladly discuss with you in private.

MY MOTTO: Enthusiasm and experience, paw in paw.

HOT DOGS
70

Shtetl Queen

What I'm Looking For: A nice Jewish CWS to settle down with. You don't have to be handsome or rich, just wise.

Why You Want To Get To Know Me: I'm an old-world dam, dutiful and ready for family life. I came here from Budapest 2 years ago and I know I will make a good wife to a good husband, a good mother to my good children.

What I'm Watching: Fiddler on the Roof, Avalon, Shoah, Une Larme dans l'Océan.

I'm Most Neurotic About: I sometimes worry that my future children might not worry enough about things when they grow up.

My Motto: Whatever life hands you, it probably belongs in the cholent.

Edgy Dam Needs Mate

WHAT I'M LOOKING FOR: Any mutt will love me when I'm in heat, but it takes a special CWS to take care of my everyday needs. I'm tired of dogs whose idea of commitment is to mark their territory and leave. I want puppies, so no backdoor dogs, please.

WHY YOU WANT TO GET TO KNOW ME: I'm a beautiful, sable-coated, silky-eared PWD with a strong mothering instinct. I've been accused of being aggressive, but I'm just trying to protect myself and my loved ones. If you get to know me, you'll find out that my bark hides a sweet disposition.

MY DREAM VACATION: Riding the rails through the Pacific Northwest with you and our litter.

WORDS I'M DYING TO HEAR: "Would you like breakfast in bed?"

MY MOTTO: Don't trifle with me.

Call Tonight!

HOT DOGS

72

I Look Good on Leather

From: dam888
Sent: Sunday, June 19, 2005 @ 12:47 PM
To: PAS
Subject: I Look Good on Leather

WHAT I'M LOOKING FOR: Shorthaired dogs with unusual scars are a particular favorite of mine. Let's discuss our histories while relaxing on the fine Corinthian leather couch my humans purchased for my personal enjoyment.

WHY YOU WANT TO GET TO KNOW ME: Even if you ignore my sleek good looks, I'm quite a catch: a good listener, a sensitive lover, and my interests include retro-modern furniture, lounge music, and body modification (I've had my tail docked).

MY PERFECT DATE: A lot of rolling around on as many different fabrics as we can find, a lot of pawing our way around town, and a lot of feeling each other up.

WHAT I'M BEGGING FOR: Ostrich meat tartar with a splash of Tabasco.

MY MOTTO: It's gotta feel good to be good.

Poundbait

From: dam45490
Sent: Tuesday, June 14, 200
@ 8:46 AM
To: C/PWS
Subject: RE: Poundbait

WHAT I'M LOOKING FOR: An older dog willing to tempt fate, who'll lavish me with attention and the finest accessories a nose can find. In other words, a sugar-doggy for this young damsel.

WHY YOU WANT TO GET TO KNOW ME: I'm coming up on my 1st birthday, and when I reach that magical age I want to be living the good life. Interests include: going to the mall, hanging out, chewing Prada shoes, getting groomed, and looking my best.

MY LEAST FAVORITE CLICHÉ: That being a Labrador somehow means you're a bimbo and, like, dumb. Like, whatever!

WHAT'S IN MY BEDROOM: No one, yet—when are you coming over?

MY MOTTO: Be careful—what we do together could land you in the pound!

COMMUNITY ACTIVIST

WHAT I'M LOOKING FOR:
Community-minded pooch who wears his heart on his collar. You're committed to the cause but not blind to your emotional needs, or those of your friends.

WHY YOU WANT TO GET TO KNOW ME: Did you know that the Elm Street dog run is slated to be demolished to make way for a children's playground!? If this sort of encroachment by the forces that be is allowed to continue we'll be drinking fetid gutter water, and puppies will be forced to play fetch in rank back alleys. The time to bite eminent domain in the ass is NOW!

HOW I'D LIKE TO CHANGE THE WORLD: Unrecycled poop will soon take over large portions of the park. I will work tirelessly to see that humans collect and redistribute this valuable asset.

WHAT'S IN MY BEDROOM: "War is bad for children and all living things" poster, 800 flyers about the playground development, and a secret horde of cheese.

MY MOTTO: Think globally, act locally.

HOT DOGS
75

Sugar and Spice and Everything Nice

WHAT I'M LOOKING FOR: You're a strong, confident, shorthaired PAS with sturdy shoulders and a mischievous side.

WHY YOU WANT TO GET TO KNOW ME: I'm sweet as a pickle, and twice as cute (thanks to my overgrown whiskers). I'm a submissive PAD (I'll roll over and show you my belly if I decide I like you), who loves all kinds of animals and goes out of her way to give them a friendly sniff.

WHAT I'M BEGGING FOR: Peppermint-flavored beef jerky (and thou!).

WHAT'S IN MY BEDROOM: My collection of teddy bears, my collection of teddies (ooh la la), and by my bedside, a guide to North American B&Bs (I do love my weekends in the country!).

MY MOTTO: I want to be your teddy bear.

Ooo La La!

Any Port in a Storm

What I'm Looking For: Randy terrier seeks large-membered PAS for rough-and-tumble, no-holds-barred, doggie-style humpin'. You are an attentive, mature lover with plenty of experience and an easygoing, fun-loving disposition. No psychos and no STDs, please—clean bill of mental and physical health a MUST.

Why You Want To Get To Know Me: I am a highly sexually evolved PWD with a LOT of love to give. I am athletic, self-confident, and looking for an energetic lover who can keep up.

What's In My Bedroom: Long-handled mop, push-broom, large Peugeot peppermill, velvet-lined four-way paw cuffs, large dog bed, and family-sized bottle of Astroglide.

My Motto: Is that a plunger in your pants, or are you just happy to see me?

Looking to Step Out a Little

WHAT I'M LOOKING FOR: A quick, no-questions-asked affair, with a like-minded CAS who's discreet and sensitive. I don't care if you're involved elsewhere, as long as our time together is our own. I'm especially interested in seeing what it's like to be with a mutt—I hear mutts do it human-style and I'd love to try that.

WHY YOU WANT TO GET TO KNOW ME: I'm in a long-term, mostly happy relationship (that's me on the left), but, as the ancients say, "a little variety prevents madness" (or at least they would have if confronted by a dog who snores like a pig in a vacuum cleaner and eats dirty socks).

MY FAVORITE PHYSICAL ACTIVITIES: Precision team fetch, puddle sploobing, changing direction when running (I'm not very good at this yet).

MY FANTASY OWNER: Meryl Streep—brains, talent, class, a woman of appetites, who could be better?

MY MOTTO: Discretion is the better part of valor.

HOT DOGS

78

Blog Dog

From: dam101
Sent: Saturday, July 2, 2005 @ 10:56 AM
To: PAS
Subject: RE: Blog Dog

WHAT I'M LOOKING FOR: You are a PAS with your own blog and a long list of websites you MUST check every 5 minutes. You know how to sex-up an email, and you average 80 WPM.

WHY YOU WANT TO GET TO KNOW ME: I may tell the world about the circumstances in which you lost your virginity a mere 2 hours after you give me that information in confidence, but I'd expect no less from you. I'm a PAD who covers a unique blend of the personal and the political.

MY PERFECT DATE: Clearly we'd both be writing up our experiences for the internet, but we'd have to be discreet, skipping off to the bathroom to take notes every once in a while. We'd have a quick dinner, and then make our excuses. You'd go straight home to upload your story only to discover I'd sent in mine from my mobile phone. Ha!

WHAT I'VE BEEN BLOGGING: My ex has had a flea bath twice this month (still no luck, sucker!), economic subsidies for dog chews are being cut by the European Union, and the President's dog was seen sharing puppy snacks with the sexy doggy diplomat from Mexico.

MY MOTTO: Honesty is my only excuse.

HOT DOG!

79

Reincarnated Lovers

WHAT I'M LOOKING FOR: We met in Paris during the heady days of the Revolution; you were Napoleon, and I was your Josephine. By the banks of the Nile, you were Caesar, and I was Cleopatra. Let's meet again and rekindle our romances.

WHY YOU WANT TO GET TO KNOW ME: This unfinished affair is bad for the soul. Let's try to make it work this time. No more hubris, no more empire-building.

WHO I'VE BEEN CHANNELING: Along with some of the great queens of history, a turnspit dog from the 13th Century, a 9th century B.C. pot-boy called Eric looking for help with his homework, and Norris, a dormouse from Devon.

IF I RULED THE WORLD: Well, I don't currently, but I have in the past, and it's a very stress-ful job without as many opportu-nities to change things as you might think.

MY MOTTO: If you're not careful, karma will come back and bite you where the hair don't grow....

Hotcha!

Lift Me Up Where I Belong

What I'm Looking For: You're a big (in stature or heart) CWS with chiseled good looks, equally at home walking at heel through the park or tearing after a tennis ball on a fashionable beachfront. No smokers, please.

Why You Want To Get To Know Me: I may look like a little moppet, but I'm an athletic PWD who can sweep you off your feet. I've got a sweet disposition, I'm lavishly affectionate, and I run competitively. I'm currently in training for my first Iron Dog triathalon.

What I'm Watching: The Way We Were, Chariots of Fire, An Officer and a Gentleman.

Worst Date Experience: Losing my date at the dog spa, and having to jog home 2 miles in the pouring rain—without company and without my blue slicker!

My Motto: A day doesn't start right without a jog around the park.

Globe-Trotting Field Tripper

From: dam2121
Sent: Sunday, June 12, 2005 @ 10:40 AM
To: PAS
Subject: RE: Globe-Trotting Field Tripper

WHAT I'M LOOKING FOR: A PAS who is well-educated and eager to share the best that the city has to offer. Did you know that over 100 dogs visit your average hydrant on any given day? Let's get together and pool our knowledge about the world around us. Looking for companionship, possibly romance.

WHY YOU WANT TO GET TO KNOW ME: I'm a robust, blonde PWD in the prime of life. I'm bookish, but as eager to take a long walk as to sit inside chewing over a great book. And, I know where to get the best pizza in the city.

MY DREAM VACATION: A long summer trek through Europe, with plenty of time to savor the sights and scents of life as it's lived in the Old Dog Country.

MY GREATEST AMBITION: To write the great canine novel.

MY MOTTO: There's something amazing around every corner.

HELP ME FIND MY MAGIC SPOT!

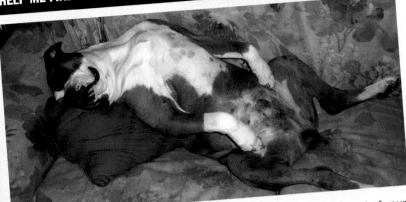

WHAT I'M LOOKING FOR: From the tip of your cold, wet nose, to the end of your enthusiastic tail, you must be a fit, toned, and sexy PAS. You like to lick a dam until she pants for mercy—but you don't stop. No lap dogs, please—I need a big dog.

WHY YOU WANT TO GET TO KNOW ME: I'm in excellent physical shape, can run down a squirrel or slow-moving SUV. I'll let you tickle my washboard abs until you get my left leg moving in crazy circles. And then it's my turn! Oh the places we will go....

WHAT'S IN MY BEDROOM: Satin sheets, a mirror on the ceiling, and Al Green playing all night long.

MY FAVORITE PHYSICAL ACTIVITIES: Crazed running through the forest underbrush following scents, followed by frenzied humping and, finally, prolonged lounging on a big sunny lawn.

MY MOTTO: Sometimes "no" means "don't stop now!"

HOT DOGS
83

Rub-a-Dub-Dub

WHAT I'M LOOKING FOR: You're an older PAS, a true gentleman with a taste for the sophisticated things in life: anchovy pizza, salmon-salad sandwiches, dry-aged road-kill—and me. We'll go out for a walk and roll in anything we want to—we

can always wash up afterwards.

WHY YOU WANT TO GET TO KNOW ME: I'm a very fastidious dam "of a certain age." I've elevated bathing to an art form, and I'm looking for someone to share my passion with. Are you ready to get wet in tandem and let me wash you behind the ears?

WORDS I'M DYING TO HEAR: "Here, darling, let me soap your back."

WHAT'S IN MY BATHROOM: Muddy Puddle facial masks, Bouillons of Bubbles: Meat Essence Bath Beads, and a set of bone-shaped loofahs.

MY MOTTO: Like Rubber Ducky, I know how to make bath time fun.

Party Animal Ready for the Next Step

From: dam357
Sent: Tuesday, July 26, 2005 @ 12:43 PM
To: CAD
Subject: RE: Party Animal Ready for the Next Step

WHAT I'M LOOKING FOR: The best I can do is to find my bed some nights. I'm looking for a helping hand getting my life under control. I smoke, I drink, and I compulsively steal shoes. I've hit bottom and need some TLC from a strong, patient CAS to climb back up. Show me you care.

WHY YOU WANT TO GET TO KNOW ME: I'm NOT looking for a masochist: If I didn't think I was worth getting to know, I wouldn't run this ad. I'm an intelligent, attractive CWD who's also danger-ously charming (but I'm warning you, so that's okay) and funny. I'm a mess, but I clean up nice.

WHAT I'M READING: *Been Down So Long It Looks Like Up to Me, Who's Afraid of Virginia Woof?, Butterfield 8.*

WHAT'S IN MY BEDROOM: You know, I can't really remember.

MY MOTTO: One step at a time (at least 'til all 12 are out of the way).

SIRES SEEKING DAMS

Hair of the Dog

WHAT I'M LOOKING FOR: I need a girlfriend like some mornings I need an aspirin and a cool bowl of water. You're a refreshing and cheerful PAD, with enough personality to distract me from the pain that follows a night of sitting under my human's chair in a bar licking beer off the floor.

WHY YOU WANT TO GET TO KNOW ME: Despite the occasional hangover, I'm a responsible and loving dog, eager to connect with others. Let's get out in the open air and get to know each other while doing something healthy. And yes, I am losing my hair a little, so my nightly Rogaine application is a must.

MY FAVORITE HANGOVER CURE: When the beer dog bites I find that a large greasy breakfast, followed by a cold dip in the toilet gets me into great shape.

WHAT I'M BEGGING FOR: Beef jerky and a little QT spent with you.

MY MOTTO: Moderation in all things— well, most things.

Hunky Stud!

HOT DOGS

Laid-Back Looking for a Lady to Lay

What I'm Looking For: A hot, sexy, and chaos-tolerant AD (P or C, don't care) who's happy to let sleeping dogs lie (in their unmade beds, even, if that's what they want to do). It would be for the best if you were a little neater than me.

Why You Want To Get To Know Me: I'm a dog's dog, the rascally sort who can't be trusted alone in the house by the humans. I'm a laid-back CWS with a good sense of humor who knows how to relax and enjoy life instead of just rushing along, never taking time to smell the hydrants.

My Favorite Human Trait: The way their faces get all blotchy and red when they're telling you not to hump your honey in their bed.

Pet Peeves: Mornings, alarm clocks, spring cleaning.

My Motto: Sleeping dogs tell no lies.

Club Pup Seeks Rave Partner

WHAT I'M LOOKING FOR: You're a C/PAD who's into neo-techno and German house music—no poseurs, no preppies, and no punked-out pooper-scoopers who don't know how to rave till the break of dawn. All the squares can go home.

WHY YOU WANT TO GET TO KNOW ME: I'm a dedicated, club-hopping, velvet-rope-jumping dance hound with a taste for E and the stamina to go all night, all day, and all night again, if I'm feeling it. I'm a sex machine. I'm a nonstop flight from here to forever—why not get yourself a first-class ticket and see the world from the dark side?

WHAT I'M BEGGING FOR: A light stick, endless bowls of purified water, premium laser show, and MDMA by the pawful.

MY DREAM VACATION: Armed with music and our love of dance, you and me and 12,000 other club dogs take Berlin for a week of nonstop Telefunken action.

MY MOTTO: The music sounds better with you.

HOT DOG!
90

CONNOISSEUR SEEKS SAME

WHAT I'M LOOKING FOR: Lovely little PAD with great aesthetic sense. Must have appreciation of art and design that goes beyond the usual Pavlovian response to objects and buildings. Your idea of a good time should include visiting art galleries.

WHY YOU WANT TO GET TO KNOW ME:
I'm a connoisseur of the finest in dog-related antiques, handling objects that are often many times older than the oldest dog living today. I'm an intellectual PAS who will take the time to share the beauty of the world with my special one.

MY FAVORITE PIECE OF DESIGN: The Frank Lloyd Wright Doghouse in San Anselmo, California.

MY GREATEST AMBITION: To create an easy way for dogs to open doors, regardless of stature. Why must there always be this bourgeois obsession with opposable thumbs?

MY MOTTO: Size is nothing—design matters.

HOT DOGS

Street Artist

WHAT I'M LOOKING FOR: A hip, downtown dam with street smarts and a sense of humor. I'm a working artist, who's found it hard to have time for a social life. You aren't overly impressed by rules, and make a good lookout.

WHY YOU WANT TO GET TO KNOW ME: I'm an up-and-coming street artist (you may have seen or smelled my work). I'm creative, a bit of a risk taker, and willing to stand up for what I believe in.

MY FAVORITE ARTWORK: Keith Haring's *Barking Dogs*.

MY GREATEST AMBITION: To leave my "tag" where the whole world will get to smell it.

MY MOTTO: Unleashed in the streets.

Love's a Deuce

From: sire6454
Sent: Thursday, June 16, 2005 @ 8:11 AM
To: PAD
Subject: Love's a Deuce

WHAT I'M LOOKING FOR: PAS seeks mature partner to hold me and hug me and call me honey. You're a PAD of good disposition and training, who's looking to take a lovable geezer in paw.

WHY YOU WANT TO GET TO KNOW ME: I've been a line judge for the USTA for 7 years now, and in my down time I like to coach the neighborhood pups, whether it's tennis ball fetching or any kind of ball fetching. Heck, I like to offer advice. And it's pretty good advice, too—I'm fair and impartial.

WHAT I'M BEGGING FOR: I'd really like to see the glass ceiling erased for dogs in sports—why, even the terminology ("bat boy, ball boy, gofer," etc.) strikes me as biased against canines.

MY GREATEST AMBITION: To see a dog tennis player, male or female, earn the number-one ranking.

MY MOTTO: I call 'em like I see 'em, and if I like you when I see you, I'll call you "sweetie."

The Postman Always Rings Twice

WHAT I'M LOOKING FOR: A tough, intelligent, slightly feral CAD, with whom this CAS can take on the human hegemony.

WHY YOU WANT TO GET TO KNOW ME: The USPS spends $10 million annually to supply its employees with mace, electric animal prods, and other aggressive anti-dog measures. We have to even the score. Let's outflank some postal service employees and teach them the meaning of respect.

WHAT I'M WATCHING: *The Postman, Mad Max, Planet of the Apes.*

WHAT I'M BEGGING FOR: Custom-made goggles to protect my eyes against pepper spray.

MY MOTTO: Just because you're paranoid doesn't mean they're not out to get you....

Call Tonight!

O Sole Mio

What I'm Looking For: I'm looking for a lover—what are you doing tonight? 'Cause tomorrow's too late.... Anyway, you're an empathetic PWD with a sincere love of timeless music and a heart open to romance.

Why You Want To Get To Know Me: I'm a hound with a heart of gold and pipes to match. I'll sing you to sleep in the evenings and announce our love in song to the entire world during the day.

My Perfect Day: I notice the kitchen door has been left open. You and I slip out of the house and tour the neighborhood until dusk, when we slip into the local opera house for an evening of glorious music. Afterward, we create dramatic tension of our own as we curl up together in our love nest....

My Greatest Ambition: To sing a capella with a pack of hunting hounds.

My Motto: It's now or never!

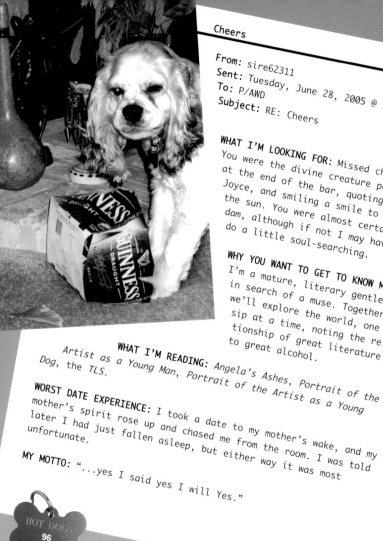

Cheers

From: sire62311
Sent: Tuesday, June 28, 2005 @ 3:34 PM
To: P/AWD
Subject: RE: Cheers

WHAT I'M LOOKING FOR: Missed chance: You were the divine creature perched at the end of the bar, quoting James Joyce, and smiling a smile to rival the sun. You were almost certainly a dam, although if not I may have to do a little soul-searching.

WHY YOU WANT TO GET TO KNOW ME: I'm a mature, literary gentleman in search of a muse. Together we'll explore the world, one sip at a time, noting the relationship of great literature to great alcohol.

WHAT I'M READING: Angela's Ashes, Portrait of the Artist as a Young Man, Portrait of the Artist as a Young Dog, the TLS.

WORST DATE EXPERIENCE: I took a date to my mother's wake, and my mother's spirit rose up and chased me from the room. I was told later I had just fallen asleep, but either way it was most unfortunate.

MY MOTTO: "...yes I said yes I will Yes."

HOT DOGS
96

JOIN MY POSSE

WHAT I'M LOOKING FOR: Sexy, soulful PWD to roll with me, living the thug life. You're a big-boned dog with back—and street smarts. I expect you to hold your own in this relationship, but don't forget who's the A-dog here.

WHY YOU WANT TO GET TO KNOW ME: I'm a stand-up PWS with mad potentiality and a pimpin' whip. Plus, I'll treat you like the honey-baby you are—you'd be crazy not to get up with this dog!

PET PEEVES: Punk dogs who front, running out of Cristal.

WHAT I'M LISTENING TO: Snoop Dogg, Maxwell, Lyrics Born.

MY MOTTO: "Bow wow wow, yippee yo yippee yay."

HOT DOGS
97

Deer Hunter

WHAT I'M LOOKING FOR: Conservative, traditional PWD who is interested in dating a solid citizen like myself. Must be open to the possibility of having pups one day, even if it's pretty far down the road.

WHY YOU WANT TO GET TO KNOW ME: I'm a veteran DEA dog who had to retire when his nose went. I can still smell a can of chili being opened a mile away, but I can no longer tell the difference between Columbian blue-flake and Peruvian "mountain rose" cocaine. I'm affable, a hard worker, and a devoted companion.

PET PEEVES: Long-haired hippie cats, bad dogs, downtime.

MY HOBBIES INCLUDE: Stalking large animals, scaring birds, treeing raccoons. Plus I do a great impression of a deer, which helps me blend in when I'm hunting.

MY MOTTO: I'd rather be fishing.

Take Me Out to the Ball Game

From: sire12
Sent: Friday, June 3, 2005 @ 8:25 AM
To: PAD
Subject: RE: Take Me Out to the Ball Game

WHAT I'M LOOKING FOR: You're a PAD who really loves baseball. For you, a perfect day is an afternoon at the ballpark, eating hotdogs and drinking beer out of a plastic cup.

WHY YOU WANT TO GET TO KNOW ME: I've got an encyclopedic knowledge of the game, from the good old days to the days of "juice" and roses—and I specialize in mascot history! Plus, I always finish what I start—I solemnly swear our love will never, ever be canceled due to rain!

WHAT I'M WATCHING: Pride of the Yankees, Field of Dreams, Bull Durham, ESPN Sports Center and Baseball Tonight.

PET PEEVE: Dogs who don't "get" statistics.

MY MOTTO: Reinstate Shoeless Joe!

Night Dogging

WHAT I'M LOOKING FOR: A really built broad who's a class act. Should be sweet and nice, unlike the usual dams I meet.

WHY YOU WANT TO GET TO KNOW ME: I'm a CAS who enjoys the nightlife, the high life, and the good life, but I'm ready for a special lady to settle down with. I'll always have dogs' night out, but it's important to have something solid to come home to, especially if you're ever thinking about puppies, which is not to say that I am, but who knows.

WHAT I'M LISTENING TO: Frank Sinatra, Louis Prima, Dean Martin.

WHAT I'D CHANGE ABOUT MYSELF: Unpaid gambling debts.

MY MOTTO: The best is yet to come.

Hunky Stud!

HOT DOGS
100

Let's Get Cookin'!

What I'm Looking For: You're a WD, with a refined palate and culinary talents. Plus, you're no stranger to a restaurant kitchen—you know how to hop to it or get out of the way!

Why You Want To Get To Know Me: I'm an up-and-coming pastry dog who just landed a pilot for a cooking show on TLC. Plus, I know how to make sweet, sweet love: I will marinate you, simmer you, baste you, and serve you up a towering plate of desire.

My Greatest Ambition: To open up my own theme restaurant. It will be based on the great bone-based dishes: Osso Buco, Leg of Lamb, and, of course, gelatin-based desserts.

What I'm Begging For: My all-time favorite comfort food is saltines spread with peanut butter.

My Motto: What's your fancy tonight?

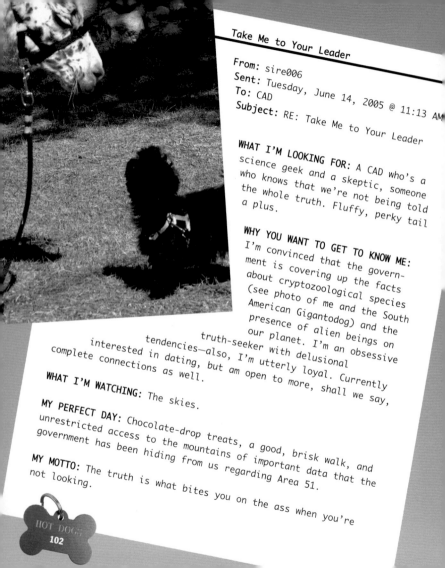

Take Me to Your Leader

From: sire006
Sent: Tuesday, June 14, 2005 @ 11:13 AM
To: CAD
Subject: RE: Take Me to Your Leader

WHAT I'M LOOKING FOR: A CAD who's a science geek and a skeptic, someone who knows that we're not being told the whole truth. Fluffy, perky tail a plus.

WHY YOU WANT TO GET TO KNOW ME: I'm convinced that the government is covering up the facts about cryptozoological species (see photo of me and the South American Gigantodog) and the presence of alien beings on our planet. I'm an obsessive truth-seeker with delusional tendencies—also, I'm utterly loyal. Currently interested in dating, but am open to more, shall we say, complete connections as well.

WHAT I'M WATCHING: The skies.

MY PERFECT DAY: Chocolate-drop treats, a good, brisk walk, and unrestricted access to the mountains of important data that the government has been hiding from us regarding Area 51.

MY MOTTO: The truth is what bites you on the ass when you're not looking.

HOT DOGS
102

PERSONALS

HELL-BENT FOR LEATHER

WHAT I'M LOOKING FOR: I'm a tough rodeo dog who's been out riding fences for a long time, and now I'm ready for a sweet little critter to run down and hog-tie. All big dams and untamed mares considered.

WHY YOU WANT TO GET TO KNOW ME: I'm a rough-and-tumble dogpoke, but I've got gentle paws and a loving disposition. After I ride you like a wild bronco, I'll treat you real good: I'll drink champagne out of your shoes and call you "ma'am."

WHAT I'M BEGGING FOR: Big, juicy steaks, fiery hot chili, baked beans.

WHAT'S IN MY BEDROOM: Just me, my horse, and the big sky.

MY MOTTO: Don't fence me in!

HOT DOGS
103

Tycoon

WHAT I'M LOOKING FOR: Self-made CAS seeks PAD, but being purebred isn't enough—you have to be well-trained too. Long hair and good table manners a must.

WHY YOU WANT TO GET TO KNOW ME: I may be a cross (not a mutt), but I'm a pure luxury mammal. Let's take an afternoon to revel in the best the park has to offer: a quick romp through some muddy puddles, a sniff or three at the dog run, and a roll in some offal.

WHAT I'M READING: *The Great Gatsby*, *The Fountainhead*, *The Art of the Deal*.

A SECRET MOST OTHERS DON'T KNOW ABOUT ME: I made my first million at the greyhound races.

MY MOTTO: Money does grow on trees.

Hottie!

HOT DOGS
104

Communicate with Outer Space!

From: sire10101
Sent: Sunday, July 3, 2005 @ 8:39 PM
To: P/CA/WD
Subject: RE: Communicate with Outer Space!

WHAT I'M LOOKING FOR: An intelligent, open-minded dog who believes that we are not alone in the universe. You are not afraid to peer into the depths of the unknown. Also, you play contract bridge.

WHY YOU WANT TO GET TO KNOW ME: I'm a successful inventor (though my work has been kept from the general public by dark forces). Also, I am an incredibly social PWS and an excellent conversationalist.

MY GREATEST ACHIEVEMENT: A small conical device (which I disguise as a party hat) that allows me to communicate with beings on other planets. Wearing two at once increases the reception.

MY PERFECT DATE: Given the off-planet intelligence I'm receiving, it might be a good idea to hide deep underground in a concrete bunker, sometime around next May. Either way, don't forget your aluminum-foil hat.

MY MOTTO: Damn it, Jim—I'm a dog, not an exobiologist!

HOT DOGS
105

Master of Camouflage

What I'm Looking For: A mysterious, slightly wild PWD, in touch with her natural self, able to work in a pack or as a lone dog. Must want children.

Why You Want To Get To Know Me: I'm a master tracker and survivalist, a disguise specialist, and I love the outdoors. When human society comes crashing down around our ears we're going to have to fend for ourselves. You can look forward to that future with confidence with me by your side.

What I'm Watching: Rambo, Red Dawn, Lost.

What's In My Bedroom: How to Survive in the Woods, a first-aid kit, Leatherman Deluxe, Bowie knife, compass, vacuum-sealed bags of gorp, water-purifying kit.

My Motto: The dogs shall inherit the earth.

Road Trip!

WHAT I'M LOOKING FOR: A quirky C/PWD to join me on life's incredible journeys (especially the car trips). Must have long tongue and smelly breath. Drooling and farting a plus.

WHY YOU WANT TO GET TO KNOW ME: I'm a fool for the open road, baby; it doesn't matter to me where we're going as long as we go, dog, go! I'm a traveling dog, a tumbleweed, a Merry Prankster! Let's stick our heads out the window and let the spittle land where it may.

WHAT I'M WATCHING: National Lampoon's Vacation, Road Trip, The Incredible Journey.

WHAT'S IN MY GLOVE COMPARTMENT: Guidebooks, beef jerky, dog biscuits, and maps.

MY MOTTO: Are we there yet? Are we? There? Yet?

Ooo La La!

HOT DOGS

Tears of a Clown

From: sire4551
Sent: Friday, July 1, 2005 @ 12:48 PM
To: PAD
Subject: RE: Tears of a Clown

WHAT I'M LOOKING FOR: Purebred Pagliacci seeks PAD with whom I can share my inner life. You're sensitive, but not overburdened with angst of your own. Believe me, there's only room for one tragicomedy around here. You're lively, enjoy a good romp with a ball, and are not afraid of big, red shoes.

WHY YOU WANT TO GET TO KNOW ME: It isn't easy being funny for a living, especially when your first wife left you for a circus strongdog. When I perform I'm surrounded by dogs who are absolutely howling with laughter, but all the while my heart is breaking inside.

WHAT I'M WATCHING: Les Enfants du Paradis, Shakes the Clown, Freaks.

WHAT'S IN MY DRESSING ROOM: Greasepaint, box of tissues, hidden bottle of vodka.

MY MOTTO: The show must go on.

HOT DOGS
108

PHEROMONE PHRENZY

WHAT I'M LOOKING FOR: You're out there, and, baby, you're a PWD in heat. I can't see you but I can feel you, and it's driving me insane. One minute I'm enjoying a quiet afternoon watching TV, the next I'm climbing out the window. They'll say I'm wearing estrus goggles, but baby you're the most beautiful dog in the world.

WHY YOU WANT TO GET TO KNOW ME: I'm smart, funny, witty, and sex-crazed. Stand still, sweetheart, while I nuzzle your posterior. Just for a second, please.... Arghh! If I can't get a piece of your sweetness, I may have to hump the couch. Or maybe the cat—again.

MY PERFECT DATE: With a running leap I launch myself off the human's head, and out through a window. I zero in on you within seconds. After a flurry of nose-rubbing and under-the-breath yelping, we make wild love. Then, we make love again at our leisure.

MOST EMBARRASSING MOMENT: I once drank a six-pack of beer while I was waiting for a limo to take me to the airport, and I don't remember all the details, but I know I never got on that flight and the cat has been awfully affectionate ever since.

MY MOTTO: If you can't be with the one you love, try the one lying next to you on the couch.

Dogski!

WHAT I'M LOOKING FOR: Fit, energetic, snow doggy for on- and off-piste adventures. No snowboarders, please.

WHY YOU WANT TO GET TO KNOW ME: You don't spend all day going up and down mountains without developing a profound understanding of life's hills and valleys. I'm a laid-back, athletic CAS of means and a love of *la vie sportif*. Don't let me slide away!

MY PERFECT DATE: We spend the day on the slopes on run after run, chasing after snowballs and stealing people's ski poles. In the evening we knock over steins of frothy lager and greedily lap it up before retiring to the hot tub in my chalet for some bubbly canine fun.

MOST EMBARRASSING MOMENT: I lost control on a double-black-diamond run once and slammed into a beginner's class—there were pups flying everywhere! Luckily, the instructor is a friend of mine, but he still uses that story to illustrate what not to do on the slopes.

MY MOTTO: Work hard, ski hard.

Let's Party!

From: sire7755
Sent: Saturday, July 16, 2005 @ 3:00 PM
To: PWDs
Subject: RE: Let's Party!

WHAT WE'RE LOOKING FOR: A pair of dogs gone wild! You are two hot and sexy PWDs who enjoy taking off your tube tops and lap dancing. Nothing is too crazy for you! Jump! Roll over! Bark with joy! If you like to party like it's spring break, contact us.

WHY YOU WANT TO GET TO KNOW US: They call us animals and for good reason! We're wild-and-crazy bachelors who always want to get the party started. Keg stands, bong loads, and naked pool Olympics.

OUR WORST FLAW: Sometimes we overdo it (see photo for a particularly rough morning after). But our human always cleans up after us, so it's totally cool if we occasionally barf on the carpet.

WHAT'S IN OUR BEDROOM: Awesome stereo, old pizza boxes, the sexiest pages from years of *Dogs Illustrated* swimsuit calendars, and a collection of dog bras.

OUR MOTTO: Chug! Chug! Chug!

The Dark Lord Awaits Us

WHAT I'M LOOKING FOR: A voluptuous collie or collie-spaniel mix, with long auburn hair. You are a PAD witch or member of a satanic cult and familiar with the rituals of the Church of Satan. No wackos, please—only serious individuals need reply.

WHY YOU WANT TO GET TO KNOW ME: I'm a hardworking priest of the local branch of the Church and, as such, enjoy certain privileges. I am an attentive and experienced sexual partner and, while past lovers have sometimes complained about the long hours a devoted devil-worshiper spends in dark prayer, nobody has ever accused me of being an unbeliever. That is, nobody who lived to tell the tale (just kidding—we strictly forbid blood rituals!).

WHAT I'M WATCHING: *The Blair Witch Project*, *The Exorcist*, *Rosemary's Baby*.

WORST LIE I EVER TOLD:
"I'm here today to talk to you about Jesus Christ."

MY MOTTO: Look with me into the globe of Nosliw—its fuzzy yellow heart beats with the rhythm of the Dark One's true knowledge!

Call Tonight!

HOT DOGS!
112

Who's That Lady?

What I'm Looking For: You're the C/PA/WD I hear scrabbling around in the next-door apartment day and night. I'm tired of fantasizing about you as I hump my human's leg when you're so close—let's chew through the walls and have an afternoon of hot, furry sex. I hope you're a yelper!

Why You Want To Get To Know Me: You've heard my bark, now check out my bite. I'm persistent, determined, and I've got the longest tongue this side of Main Street. Hobbies include pacing.

What I'm Watching: *Home Alone, The Girl Next Door, Behind the Green Door.*

I'm Most Neurotic About: Closed doors. I mean, what's that all about? What are they doing in there?

My Motto: If curiosity killed the cat, color me curious!

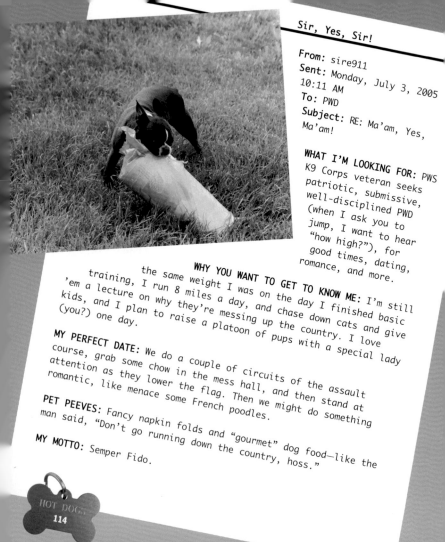

Sir, Yes, Sir!

From: sire911
Sent: Monday, July 3, 2005 10:11 AM
To: PWD
Subject: RE: Ma'am, Yes, Ma'am!

WHAT I'M LOOKING FOR: PWS K9 Corps veteran seeks patriotic, submissive, well-disciplined PWD (when I ask you to jump, I want to hear "how high?"), for good times, dating, romance, and more.

WHY YOU WANT TO GET TO KNOW ME: I'm still the same weight I was on the day I finished basic training, I run 8 miles a day, and chase down cats and give 'em a lecture on why they're messing up the country. I love kids, and I plan to raise a platoon of pups with a special lady (you?) one day.

MY PERFECT DATE: We do a couple of circuits of the assault course, grab some chow in the mess hall, and then stand at attention as they lower the flag. Then we might do something romantic, like menace some French poodles.

PET PEEVES: Fancy napkin folds and "gourmet" dog food—like the man said, "Don't go running down the country, hoss."

MY MOTTO: Semper Fido.

HOT DOGS
114

HOT DIGGITY DOG

WHAT I'M LOOKING FOR: Hot dog with extra mustard seeks mature, long-haired PAD with plenty of self-confidence and a sense of humor. You: the hot toasted buns; me: the hot dog inside.

WHY YOU WANT TO GET TO KNOW ME: Because I'm an available, single CWS, and at our age, there aren't many of us with the stamina (not to mention working equipment) to give a dam what she needs. Oh, I know the pups want us to just quietly fade away in an old dogs' home, but that's never going to happen here as long as THIS hot dog can still do a one-legged push-up.

MY DREAM VACATION: We are offered the use of the Oscar Mayer Hot Dog car for a month, so we drive across the country in the summer, taking in BBQs, ball games, and county fairs.

WHAT I'M BEGGING FOR: Franks, wieners, wurst, sausages, saveloys, Coney Island red hots—all of which is to say, hot dogs.

MY MOTTO: Grill me 'til I plump up, baby!

HOT DOGS

115

Love You Like a Hurricane

WHAT I'M LOOKING FOR: Energetic CWS seeks CAD to be the calm at the center of my hurricane. You're generous with your emotions, a spirited, confident dog with a great deal of patience.

WHY YOU WANT TO GET TO KNOW ME:
I'm a little erratic and my moods can swing from high to low with little warning, but when the emotional barometric pressure does drop, look out: it's gale-force happiness and four-on-the-floor rainbows while the weather holds!

MY BIGGEST DISAPPOINTMENT: No one will give a dog a tattoo.

MY GREATEST AMBITION: To ride across the country in the sidecar of a motorbike, chasing tornados.

MY MOTTO: When the weather's wet, wear your rubbers!

Abominable Snow Hound Seeks Bitty Bombshell

From: sire95678
Sent: Tuesday, July 19, 2005 @ 9:49 AM
To: PWD
Subject: RE: Abominable Snow Hound Seeks Bitty Bombshell

WHAT I'M LOOKING FOR:
You're an attractive PWD, a maximum 18 inches tall, who loves playing outdoors, especially in the snow. Hot cocoa by the fireplace is your idea of a great evening, but you still like to get out there and party with the hounds in the deep snow.

WHY YOU WANT TO GET TO KNOW ME: I'm a PWS with a serious addiction to the snow-bum lifestyle. If you can simultaneously be my soul mate and keep my wild side alive, I'll pull your sled for eternity or until I drop dead in my traces, whichever comes first.

A SECRET MOST OTHERS DON'T KNOW ABOUT ME: In the summer I like to open the fridge with my nose and rest my head on the vegetable crisper.

WHAT'S IN MY BEDROOM: Tiny insulated barrels of hot toddies, Piney Essence air freshener, NASTAR Certificate noting "Best Time, Jan. 27, Bitch Hill, VT," and a waterbed heated to body temperature—a perfect 101 degrees.

MY MOTTO: Life's the Iditarod—run like hell or the snow demons will swallow you for breakfast!

HOT DOGS
117

A Brewski, a Ball Game, and Thou

WHAT I'M LOOKING FOR: Easygoing PAS seeks dam of any breed for long hours of watching TV, possible long-term relationship. You don't mind fetching beer, and you can talk sports with the guys. When the others go for a walk, you'd rather stay behind and cuddle on the couch. You make great onion dip.

WHY YOU WANT TO GET TO KNOW ME: Ladies, what you see is what you get—and what you see is The Little Couch Potato That Could! I may be lazy, but I've got a lot of love to share with the right dam. And I know when to put down the remote and give my baby the lovin' she deserves.

MY THREE BIGGEST TURN-ONS: A come-from-behind victory for the underdog; stretching out on the bed after a long day of TV; Newfoundlands.

MY PERFECT DAY: First of all, it's Sunday—football all day! We raid the fridge and watch some pigskin abuse while munching raw sausage and guacamole; a few beers, a few great plays, and who knows? Maybe a touchdown in the bedroom?

MY MOTTO: Go Bulldogs! B-U-L-L-D-O-G-S!

Call Tonight!

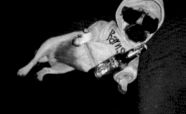

HOT DOGS
118

Sk8te or Die!

What I'm Looking For: Thrasher dams, period. I need a bitch who's as comfortable on four wheels as four paws, who's into half-pipes, nosegrinds, ollies, frontside switches, 720s, and generally getting vert. No poseurs and no goofy-foots (yeah, you know who you are).

Why You Want To Get To Know Me: I don't compromise and I don't apologize. If you're looking for the quiet life, go to church; but if you live to skate and skate to live, then let's hook up.

My Favorite Skate Trick: The Dew Claw Dippie: You sidle up to some dude's skateboard when he's not looking, jump on, and take off! "A dog stole my skateboard!" Right! Who's going to believe that?

A Surprising Fact About Me: My mom was a police dog—we had some beef when I was a teenager, but now we're chill.

My Motto: Dogtown rules!

HOT DOGS

119

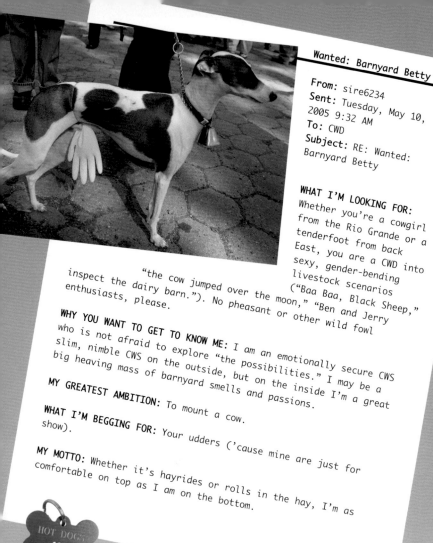

Wanted: Barnyard Betty

From: sire6234
Sent: Tuesday, May 10, 2005 9:32 AM
To: CWD
Subject: RE: Wanted: Barnyard Betty

WHAT I'M LOOKING FOR: Whether you're a cowgirl from the Rio Grande or a tenderfoot from back East, you are a CWD into sexy, gender-bending livestock scenarios ("Baa Baa, Black Sheep," "the cow jumped over the moon," "Ben and Jerry inspect the dairy barn."). No pheasant or other wild fowl enthusiasts, please.

WHY YOU WANT TO GET TO KNOW ME: I am an emotionally secure CWS who is not afraid to explore "the possibilities." I may be a slim, nimble CWS on the outside, but on the inside I'm a great big heaving mass of barnyard smells and passions.

MY GREATEST AMBITION: To mount a cow.

WHAT I'M BEGGING FOR: Your udders ('cause mine are just for show).

MY MOTTO: Whether it's hayrides or rolls in the hay, I'm as comfortable on top as I am on the bottom.

HOT DOGS
120

SALTY DOG

WHAT I'M LOOKING FOR: I'm looking for a CWD with sea legs and stamina, who can hunker down with the crew if need be, but knows how to behave like a lady on shore. Must be willing to get wet.

WHY YOU WANT TO GET TO KNOW ME: I'm a CAS, born to the sea, a rascally cove, a real pirate doggy, and I've got a tongue longer and wigglier than an eel. And, I can shakedown so hard the next three docks over get drenched.

BEST VACATION EVER: Sailing between the islands off the coast of Maine. There's a bone buried for us to find on most of them now, for when I go back with my special high-seas dam—could it be you?

WHAT'S IN MY BEDROOM: Fish guts, twine, bait & tackle.

MY MOTTO: If you don't catch them, you can't throw them back.

HOT DOGS

Conjugal Visitor Sought

From: sire3478221
Sent: Sunday, July 17, 2005 10:35 AM
To: P/CAD
Subject: RE: Conjugal Visitor Sought

WHAT I'M LOOKING FOR: I'm looking for a wild-at-heart P/CAD with space in her life for a soon-to-be ex-con with a heart of gold.

WHY YOU WANT TO GET TO KNOW ME: I'm a world-class escape artist, with many prison breaks to my name. While I'm currently incarcerated, I'm planning a break from the yard. My fluffy good looks belie a, dare I say it, dogged determination.

WHAT I'M WATCHING: *The Great Escape, Stalag 13, Con Air, The Rock.*

WHAT I'M GOING TO DO WHEN I GET OUT: Eat leftover chicken from the mini-mall garbage dumpster, run across Main Street, bark at the cops, and meet you behind the Starlight Motel for the best night of your life.

WORST LIE I EVER TOLD: "I don't know where the bones are buried!"

MY MOTTO: They ain't built a joint that can hold me yet.

Downward Dog Seeks Fellow Traveler

WHAT I'M LOOKING FOR: Inwardly beautiful and deeply spiritual P/CAD who recognizes that there is more to life than the acquisition of chew toys and the endless pursuit of kibble.

WHY YOU WANT TO GET TO KNOW ME: Yoga has given me extraordinary suppleness and a mental and physical agility that permeates all aspects of my life. I have mastered countless positions and I would like to share them with you.

HOW I RELAX WHEN I'M NOT RELAXING: I like swimming, hanging out in cafés (though I'm strictly a green-tea dog), and eating tofu outside the yoga studio.

IF I WASN'T A DOG I'D LIKE TO BE: I have long admired the mongoose for its lithe physicality and thoughtful warrior spirit.

MY MOTTO: Life is a breathing exercise.

Black Forest King Seeks Fairy Queen

WHAT I'M LOOKING FOR: A special PAD with skills in the dark arts to explore the black torment of the soul. Must have OWN chew toys, as I come from a plane of existence where it is forbidden to share.

WHY YOU WANT TO GET TO KNOW ME: I am a 17th-level sorcerous PAS whose magic is powerful, and not always white. Beware my power and come to me only if your spirit is pure.

MY PERFECT DATE: We visit the dark places of the earth together, scamper through the ruined castles of Ireland, run like wolves through dark German forests, and rage like beasts possessed (especially in the waiting room of Dr. Alphonse Gillespie, DVM).

WHAT'S IN MY BEDROOM: My bedroom is draped in black velvet that prevents the sun's light from penetrating. It is illuminated with a single black candle that gives off the musty odor of old bones.

MY MOTTO: "Come to me, O creatures of the night!"

Call Tonight!

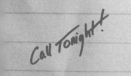

HOT DOGS
124

Let's Hit the Road

What I'm Looking For: A one night stand with a hot-blooded, hobo-lovin' CWD. I'm always on the go so I make no commitments, but I've been traveling so long that it's been almost 3 weeks since I was with a bitch.

Why You Want To Get To Know Me: I've been on the road—hitch-hiking and riding the rails—since I was a pup. It's an up-and-down lifestyle, but I've found that my giving and trusting nature is amply repaid. Not to brag or anything, but I've been with thousands of dams across the country and I know how to make 'em howl.

What I'm Reading: *On the Road*, by Jack Kerouac, *Even Cowgirls Get the Blues*, by Tom Robbins, and *Blue Highways*, by William Least Heat-Moon.

What's In My Bedroom: The contents of the continental states of America, from the wide Pacific sea to the cold Atlantic, and all points in-between.

My Motto: Brash and bold, of no fixed abode.

Dirty Dog

From: sire999
Sent: Monday, July 18, 2005 @ 3:13 PM
To: CAD
Subject: RE: Dirty Dog

WHAT I'M LOOKING FOR: You are a CAD who likes it dirty and can't wait to jump in the sack, no matter how long since I last bathed. Any mud-wrestlers out there? Call me!

WHY YOU WANT TO GET TO KNOW ME: I'm a CAS who likes to live life to its fullest, regardless of any obstacles. I have a steady job as a land surveyor, working for the human who lives in my house, and there's plenty of room to expand my operation. Could you be my partner, on the ground and in the mud?

WORST DATE EXPERIENCE: It was with a white poodle bound for the local dog show and I showed up, as usual, covered in mud. When I began sniffing her butt, her humans nearly had a heart attack. She was immediately pulled away, which suited me just fine!

IF I WASN'T A DOG I'D LIKE TO BE: If I wasn't a dog, I'd probably want to be...a dog! What can I say? Dogs have more fun than the other animals.

MY MOTTO: I never met a swamp I didn't want to dredge—or a dirty dam I didn't want to wrap my legs around!

PERSONAL

LOOKING FOR A HIGHLAND LASS

WHAT I'M LOOKING FOR: You are a spirited PWD who likes misty moors, clan gatherings, fetching the caber, and the occasional wee dram on a night that's dank and dreary.

WHY YOU WANT TO GET TO KNOW ME: I may be a wee fella, but I'm a dog among dogs, proficient in sheep-harrying, heel-nipping, and calling the humans home from the pub. Exceptionally strong forepaws provide non-slip traction on wet stone surfaces AND a firm grip during love-making. And, lass, trust me: nothing's worn under the kilt save me sword!

WHAT I'M WATCHING: *Greyfriar's Bobby, Local Hero, Brigadoon.*

WHAT I'M BEGGING FOR: Haggis, Black Bun, Irn-Bru.

MY MOTTO: *Nemo me impune lacessit* ("No one provokes me with impunity.").

I'll Get Medieval on Your Hindquarters

WHAT I'M LOOKING FOR: A lady-in-waiting who shares my enthusiasm for the world of the medieval court (from its deadly intrigue to its colorful pageantry) and has an interest in historically accurate consensual chastisement. No Victorian lapdogs, please.

WHY YOU WANT TO GET TO KNOW ME: I'm a knave, a varlet, a jester, a fool—for your love! Wench, join me in my frolick. Also, I have my own stockade, which is perfect for light S&M and the occasional time-out.

WHAT I'M WATCHING: *Monty Python and the Holy Grail, Kingdom of Heaven, A Lion in Winter, Bill and Ted's Excellent Adventure.*

WHAT'S IN MY BEDROOM: Bells, wine bladder, boots of shiny leather, a chain mail dog bed, and a suit of armor.

MY MOTTO: The renaissance fair is neither fair nor a renaissance!

Lady Soma, Come to Me!

From: sire1056
Sent: Wednesday, July 6, 2005 @ 6:03 PM
To: PAD
Subject: RE: Lady Soma, Come to Me!

WHAT I'M LOOKING FOR: You're a PAD who frequently thinks to herself, "a little shut-eye would be nice." If you're like me, the words "fast-paced" and "life" have no business sharing space in the same sentence. Care to share a siesta with me?

WHY YOU WANT TO GET TO KNOW ME: Easygoing to a fault, I'm a happy, snoozy PAS who hardly snores at all. And while I put in serious hours on the bed, it's not just sleep, sleep, sleep, if you know what I mean.

MY HOBBIES INCLUDE: Resting, napping, getting 40 winks, taking a load off, snoozing, and relaxing (with occasional breaks for chowing down and fornicating).

WHAT'S IN MY BEDROOM: A Hyperion 2800 fleece day-bed, a sheep-skin cozy, and "King Nap," a wicker all-season sleeping throne.

MY MOTTO: The world is my bedroom, and my bedroom is the world.

Mush, Baby, Mush!

WHAT I'M LOOKING FOR: A special PAD to get the sled of life moving. You're a team player, who knows that if we all pull together, the job gets done. You're single-minded and don't mind following directions. No three-legged bitches, please.

WHY YOU WANT TO GET TO KNOW ME: I've been the lead dog on a number of successful sled teams, I sleep comfortably in the snow, and rise before dawn (sometimes 6 months before dawn). I'm driven and focused, but once the job is done I like to kick back, relax, and bite my friends in a friendly way. I like to spend my time off in Aruba (see picture).

WHAT I'M READING/LISTENING TO: *Call of the Wild* and *White Fang*, by Jack London, "Don't Eat the Yellow Snow," by Frank Zappa.

WHAT'S IN MY BEDROOM: Snow goggles, cured seal skin, salmon jerky, can of Sterno.

MY MOTTO: There's no place like Nome.

Call Tonight!

HOT DOGS
130

Missed Chance!

What I'm Looking For:
Southwest Beach, October 14, 2004:
I was wearing a goofy sweater; you
were the PWD wearing a bow in her
hair. Our eyes met as the waves
crashed, but when I tried to smell
your butt I was dragged away by
"she who must be obeyed." This
photo shows me as I looked after
3 nights with no sleep, thinking of
you.

*Why You Want To Get To
Know Me:* I'm a loyal, alert,
and sexy CAS. And when someone who loves me gives me a
present, I wear it no matter what. And I never give up—
not on you, not on me.

My Greatest Ambition: To swim with the dolphins. I'm currently at work
trying to crack the code of high-pitched whistles with which they communicate.

My Perfect Date: We share a lobster roll and then go for a quiet run along the
beach. As the sun sets we conclude our unfinished business, nestled in the dunes.

My Motto: It was meant to be—let's fulfill our destiny!

Take a Gamble on Me

From: sire5115
Sent: Friday, July 8, 2005 @ 9:43 PM
To: CAD
Subject: RE: Take a Gamble on Me

WHAT I'M LOOKING FOR: Dogged loyalty, quirky humor, and a unique outlook all rolled into one sexy CAD. Enthusiasm for poker, or at least a tolerance for beer, cigars, and the possibility of financial ruin (just kidding, I'm good) a plus.

WHY YOU WANT TO GET TO KNOW ME: Take me as I am—a dog in midlife with a serious gambling jones—and you'll find a lot to love. I'll have you drooling with laughter, I'm generous and thoughtful, and I like to share the good life.

WHAT I'M WATCHING: The Sting, The Color of Money, World Championship Poker.

MY FAVORITE ARTWORK: Without a doubt the masterful "A Friend in Need," by Cassius Marcellus "Cash" Coolidge, showing the faithful bulldog slipping his bud an ace under the table.

MY MOTTO: "Never count your money when you're sitting at the table."

HOT DOGS
132

PERSONALS

DESPERATE HOUSEPETS DATING SERVICE

LET'S JITTERBUG!

WHAT I'M LOOKING FOR: I've seen it all on the streets, but I haven't seen you, baby—where you been? You: be sweet, sensitive CAD, and one helluva dancer—it's 4/4 all the time and the band just won't let up!

WHY YOU WANT TO GET TO KNOW ME: I'm built for speed, not comfort, but if you can hang on, it will be a wild ride. My big secret: under my *muy loco* exterior lurks a sensitive soul. I always come when the music of love calls, but will I get an 'attaboy from you?

WHAT I'M WATCHING: *Zoot Suit Riots* (an A&E documentary), *Dirty Dancing*, *Shall We Dance?*

WHAT'S IN MY BEDROOM: Picture of mom, zoot suits (one for every day of the week), jar of Dippity-Do, hair iron, extra clips for my .45—Uncle Sam's boys want a piece of me!

MY MOTTO: *¡Bailemos tango, chica!*

HOT DOG

133

Ballerz Wanted

WHAT I'M LOOKING FOR: Sweetness, I've been to every playground in town looking for you: a CWD who knows the difference between an alley-oop and a windmill dunk. You're a sexy, one-hound bitch with junk in her trunk and a weakness for bad boyz like me.

WHY YOU WANT TO GET TO KNOW ME: I'm a star forward PAS who brings his A-game to every encounter with a female. I will always treat you with respect, especially when I get with you where I got home-court advantage and show you some of my secret moves.

WHAT I'M WATCHING: *White Dogs Can't Jump*, *The White Shadow* (on DVD), *ESPN SportsCenter*.

WHAT'S IN MY BEDROOM: My Adidas, my Timbaz (for off-the-court romancing), and my designer sweat suits.

MY MOTTO: I like to take it to the hole every time, baby!

Revolution Now!

From: sire1917
Sent: Sunday, May 1, 2005
@ 8:00 AM
To: C/PAD
Subject: RE: Revolution Now!

WHAT I'M LOOKING FOR: Are you tired of spending your weekends chasing our oppressed feline brothers? Ever thought there might be more to life than the dog-eat-dog everyday existence? You're a committed, hardworking C/PAD. Together we'll overthrow the evil hegemonic humanigarchy.

WHY YOU WANT TO GET TO KNOW ME: I'm a CAS who refuses to accept that the dog's position in history is underneath the table, begging for scraps. I want to find the person who neutered me and cut off his balls—let's see how he likes it! Did I mention I have a vengeful streak?

WHAT I'M READING: *Animal Revolution, No Logo, Animal Farm.*

MY MOST REVOLUTIONARY ACT: To prevent my humans from participating in the oppressive exploitation of animals for food, I liberate any sausages they buy and consume them to honor the spirit of our dead brothers.

MY MOTTO: Rise up—you've nothing to lose but your leashes.

Lonesome Ivy Leaguer

WHAT I'M LOOKING FOR: Sleek, charming, intellectual CAD, with cosmopolitan tastes. Kennel Club certified baccalaureate or higher.

WHY YOU WANT TO GET TO KNOW ME: Personal ads are my last resort; neither the telephone nor I enjoyed phone sex very much, and for dogs, "speed dating" is fraught with dangers. It's messy, humans show an uncanny ability to get in the way, and any degree of success often results in savage attacks by jealous, rejected suitors. And while I don't like to brag, I manage the 401-K9 Portfolio at TD Waterhouse.

MY PERFECT DATE: We'd attend a concert in the park, making a light supper from the smorgasbord of picnic baskets there. Then we'd return home, listen to an entertaining lecture from my humans, and see where the evening leads us. Destination: romance?

WHAT'S IN MY BEDROOM: Antique family dog-bed (badly in need of some restoration, I'm afraid), my P.G. Wodehouse collection, a large pile of *The New York Review of Books* upon which I do a lot of my thinking, Blackberry wireless (the market is 24/7 these days).

MY MOTTO: *Lux et veritas.*

Call Tonight!

Married But Looking

What I'm Looking For:
I'm married (I'm the PAS on the right), but I'm looking for a little extra love on the side. Call me a scoundrel, a scamp, or a cur if you will, but I know there's an adventurous PAD out there looking for relationship-free thrills. If you're a sexy PAD who isn't uptight about long-term commitment, we should get together.

Why You Want To Get To Know Me: I'm a youthful PAS with a great body, and love to spare. Our liaisons will be brief and fulfilling, and all that sneaking around might just add a sexy *je ne sais quoi* to our relationship.

What I'm Driving: My human owns a bright, fire-hydrant-red Porsche convertible. She admits that my presence in the back seat is pretty much the only thing that keeps her under or near the speed limit. Wanna go for a ride sometime when my ol' dam is out of town?

What's In My Bedroom: We won't be visiting my bedroom, of course, but the alley behind the Seven-11 is extremely well appointed and ripe with a myriad of excellent odors.

My Motto: Youth isn't going to get wasted on this youngster!

Gadfly Seeks Gadflypaper

From: sire7
Sent: Sunday, June 5, 2005 @ 1:25 AM
To: PWD
Subject: RE: Gadfly Seeks Gadflypaper

WHAT I'M LOOKING FOR: I'd like to meet an organized and commitment-minded, younger PWD with refined good looks. I'm a creative PWS, but need help keeping focused, finishing projects, and not eating the indoor plants (it's unseemly, I know, but they're so tasty).

WHY YOU WANT TO GET TO KNOW ME: I've inherited aristocratic good looks, a glossy, luxuriant coat, and a calm, even temperament from my parents (Doncaster Glenmorangie Mansonchester Balvenie and Matilda Bedfordshire Hideyhole Knockando). Oh, and they left me a tidy little sum, too—hurry up and help me get on a budget before there's naught left but lint.

MY LEAST FAVORITE MOVIE: Best in Show. They ridiculed purebred dogs working at the top of their profession, and what's so horribly unfair is that the wretched curs never had a chance to speak for themselves!

MY MOTTO: My trust fund keeps me sane.

DON'T MAKE ME BEG

WHAT I'M LOOKING FOR: You embody the freewheeling spirit of the 1970s and are no stranger to occasional recreational drug use. You're an easygoing C/PAD, interested in exploring your spiritual and sexual self, and occasionally enjoy a recreational spin, chasing your tail until you are really, really, dizzy.

WHY YOU WANT TO GET TO KNOW ME: Come and lose yourself in my green-gray eyes. I find myself fascinating, and I know you will, too. Oh, and don't forget to bring your boogie shoes.

WHAT I'M BEGGING FOR: Baked camembert, quiche, fondue.

WHAT'S IN MY BEDROOM: A sunken, purple-velvet dog bed, *The Best of AM Gold* on quadraphonic eight-track.

MY MOTTO: Looking forward to midnight.

HOT DOGS

139

Bookends

WHAT WE'RE LOOKING FOR: Old friends. We're two retired widowers looking to meet some PADs our own age for leisurely rambles and long naps.

WHY YOU WANT TO GET TO KNOW US: If our advancing years haven't made us wiser—and no one who witnessed our behavior at the old dogs' home Christmas party last year would suggest that they have—at the very least our age has made us more mellow. Some days we don't even bother to bark at the postman.

WHAT WE'RE WATCHING: Our intake of fat, sodium, carbohydrates, and protein. Boy. We still chew on bones, though (and hope you do, too, ha ha).

OUR PERFECT DATE: Underneath the porch of the old post office is nice and cool in the summer, and we could easily spend, oh, 5 or 6 hours lying there watching the world go by. Then, when the blood sugar level is just right, perhaps a bit of conjugation?

OUR MOTTO: Older is bolder.

HOT DOGS
140

Putting On My White Tie

From: sire10
Sent: Saturday, July 9, 2005 @ 6:30 PM
To: PWD
Subject: RE: Putting On My White Tie

WHAT I'M LOOKING FOR: Fred calling Ginger: urbane, witty, man-about-town seeks slinky dance partner for good times and romantic exploration. My ideal dam can do everything I can do, backwards, and in heels.

WHY YOU WANT TO GET TO KNOW ME: I'm a PWS of the old school, a gentlehound brought up to expect that little bit extra—with the world. I'll treat you as a lady should be treated—with courtesy, chivalry, and the occasional dip at the waist.

WHAT I'M WATCHING: *Top Hat, Flying Down to Rio, The Barkleys of Broadway.*

WORDS I'M DYING TO HEAR: "You lead; I'll follow."

MY MOTTO: Put one foot in front of the other, the other, and that last one and soon you'll be dancing across the floor!

Safety First

WHAT I'M LOOKING FOR: Mature PAD who is meticulous and takes care of her mental and physical health. No diseases or genital defects, please. Must wash paws after going to the bathroom. You know that safe and sane can be sexy, too.

WHY YOU WANT TO GET TO KNOW ME: I'm a vet-certified healthy PAS with a good head on his shoulders. I've seen too many dog-run relationships fall apart because dogs weren't playing safe. It's all very well to say "lie down with dogs, get up with fleas," but it doesn't have to be that way. Parasitic vermin are NOT a natural side effect of dating.

I'M MOST NEUROTIC ABOUT: Nothing annoys me as much as a dog who shakes off excess moisture after he or she comes into a house—dry off outside, for pete's sake!

MY PERFECT DATE: We meet at the dog groomer's for their special spa treatment, we have a quiet Japanese meal (cooked fish only, please!), and take a slow and sensible walk home, where we will proceed to engage in thoroughly enjoyable coitus.

MY MOTTO: Get fixed or wear your jimmy hat!

Call Tonight!

HOT DOGS
142

Observant Mensch

What I'm Looking For:
Nice, well-brought-up dam, a bit like mom but not too much. Must be able to pop out the pups and throw together a good matzoh-based meal.

Why You Want To Get To Know Me: I'm polite, and good to my mother. I went to Hebrew school as a puppy, I have a good job, and know how to blow the shofar. I'll take our relationship seriously, and always listen to your side of the story. I've been on the dog run dating scene for too long, and it's time to settle down.

My Favorite Meal:
Sunday brunch, with fresh bagels, cream cheese, lox, and the *New York Times* crossword puzzle.

I'm Most Neurotic About: Frozen bagels. Those things taste like cardboard donuts, and I wouldn't feed them to a human.

My Motto: I'm a *meshuganah* in the bedroom.

HOT DOGS

143

From: sire563
Sent: Tuesday, July 19, 2005 @ 12:03 PM
To: CWD
Subject: RE: Here's Johnny!

WHAT I'M LOOKING FOR: Nothing can hold you back from what you want, and you need instant gratification all the time. If you want to hump something, you hump whatever's nearby—another dog, the ottoman, a human leg, whatever. And if a tasty morsel lies just beyond that fence, you'll jump it. You're a bad-ass, just like me. Breed is unimportant—just being a bitch is good enough for me.

WHY YOU WANT TO GET TO KNOW ME: I'm a resourceful CWS who lets nothing stand in my way. I have an exceptional nose and I attended Boy Scout meetings with my human's son, so I know how to survive in the wilderness should we ever have to go on the lam.

WHAT I'M READING: Cujo, The Shining, How to Get What You Want.

WHAT'S IN MY BEDROOM: L.L. Bean "Sport" dog bed, table scraps, a chainsaw.

MY MOTTO: Never beg, never give up, never say die (unless it's to some uppity dog whose throat you just happened to rip out).

HOT DOGS!
144

THESE COLORS DON'T RUN

WHAT I'M LOOKING FOR: You're a Democratic dam who lives within one-day's driving distance of western Tennessee. All other details (breed, working reproductive organs, etc.) unimportant. Sorry, no Jehovah's Witnesses.

WHY YOU WANT TO GET TO KNOW ME: Like you, I'm a blue-blooded, Yankee Doodle Dandy, even though I live in a rambling, ranch-style mansion in the great Red Middle. Despite my French ancestry and political leanings, I get along quite well with my GOP neighbors: They respect the fact that I'm a cold-blooded, gopher-killing machine, regardless of party affiliation. Plus, my humans have an Olympic-sized lap pool.

WHAT I'M READING: *Bushwhacked: Life in George W. Bush's America, Lies and the Lying Liars Who Tell Them: A Fair and Balanced Look at the Right, Freakonomics: A Rogue Economist Explores the Hidden Side of Everything.*

WHAT'S IN MY BEDROOM: TiVo, keys to my pickup, and my blue bandanna.

MY MOTTO: Am I the only one out here who likes to pee on the bushes?

HOT DOGS
145

Cats Have Nine Lives; We Only Have One

WHAT I'M LOOKING FOR: My cat friends like to boast (when they're not talking about their therapists) about their multiple lives. Multiple personalities seems more like it, but you know how cats are. Anyway, I know that I have only one life to live and I don't want to live it unloved. You're a sleek, charming huntress who looks fierce, but has a twinkle in her eye.

WHY YOU WANT TO GET TO KNOW ME: I'm a loving, athletic dog who's at her happiest when she's running with a pack.

MY DREAM VACATION: Hunting lemmings above the Arctic Circle with you.

MY BIGGEST FEAR: I fear that one day I may have to get into a fight when some bigoted dog badmouths cats—I don't like violence, but a dam's got to protect her loved ones.

MY MOTTO: One life, live it large.

Scandinavian Snow Dog

From: dam10001
Sent: Monday, July 18, 2005 @ 4:13 PM
To: PAD
Subject: RE: Scandinavian Snow Dog

WHAT I'M LOOKING FOR:
Hot sporty PAD, with an interest in winter sports, outside activity, saunas, rolling in the snow naked, and being lightly exfoliated with birch twigs (it's so stimulating!).

WHY YOU WANT TO GET TO KNOW ME: I'm new to the world of saunas but I'm an enthusiastic convert. Let's spend an afternoon sweating out the toxins before a refreshing frolic in the snow. Afterward, we'll relax in the hot tub and share a shot of aquavit.

BEST PIECE OF DESIGN: Ericsson phones, Volvo cars, and Swedish meatballs.

IF I WASN'T A DOG I'D LIKE TO BE: A magnificent elk.

MY MOTTO: Roll with the snow dogs and you're in good company.

Let's Tear This Playhouse Down!

WHAT I'M LOOKING FOR: I'm a rrrrriot dog, looking to break out of the padded cell of her existence. If I see another pink-ribboned stuffed toy, I'm going to eat it. (Check pic if you think I'm joking.) What I want to see more of is you, a tough CWD with curly hair and a bad attitude.

WHY YOU WANT TO GET TO KNOW ME: I may look like your typical suburban dog, but I'm a wild child. I'm into canine graffiti, extreme sports (running up and down the stairs really fast), and howling to really loud music or at garbage trucks.

WHAT I'M LISTENING TO: "The Drama You've Been Craving," "Rebel Rebel," "Fell in Love with a Girl."

MY GREATEST AMBITION: To kick over my dog bed, gnaw through the walls of the house, and head for California.

MY MOTTO: Never, ever do what you should—do what you want instead.

Hotcha!

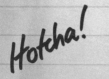

HOT DOGS

150

Biker Babe

What I'm Looking For: Butch dam seeks lipstick lesbian. You're a loving and energetic PAD ~~with a sense~~ of style who (enjoys taking care) of her partner. And you know how to ride on the back of a chopper.

Why You Want To Get To Know Me: I'm a good dog, with simple needs. I would prefer to spend the day puttering around the house and working on special projects rather than go to parties and be social. I do drive a hog, of course, and cherish my tree-rattling rides through the countryside. But shake me up a bit, I need a change.

Most Embarrassing Moment: Allowing the postman to pet me— disgusting breeder!

What's In My Bedroom: Official NY Liberty WNBA jersey, plaid blanket, studded black leather panniers, and my George Eliot collection.

My Motto: Get your motor running, head out for the dog run.

Witch Dog

WHAT I'M LOOKING FOR: Tarot-reading, Zodiac-aware PAD, with an open mind about those forces in the world we don't truly understand (like television and can openers). You're a sexy dog, but dignified, in her middle years.

WHY YOU WANT TO GET TO KNOW ME: You should know that I can never be in a relationship without consulting my coven. However, you should see this as an opportunity for growth on your part. Also, I'm sensitive, I care about your needs, and I have a great sense of humor.

WHAT I'M WATCHING: Buffy the Vampire Slayer, Charmed, Bewitched.

WHAT'S IN MY BEDROOM: Runes, crystals, and a lot of sticks I've found that are heavy with natural magic.

MY MOTTO: What's in the cards?

HOT DOGS
152

DIAL D FOR DOGGY

WHAT I'M LOOKING FOR: I'm waiting for your call. I know you're out there somewhere: an attractive, intellectually curious CAD who's technologically adept. You like conversation, quiet companionship, and smiling at the small things in life. I've found that cross-breeds are as a rule more resourceful and have fewer hang-ups. Sorry, purebreds!

WHY YOU WANT TO GET TO KNOW ME: I'm a large and fit CAD with a comfortable life, good friends, and interesting hobbies. What I don't have is a smart romantic companion to share the good times with.

MY HOBBIES INCLUDE: Rotisserie League fetch, dining al fresco, collecting antiques (I specialize in telephones).

PET PEEVE: Telemarketers!

MY MOTTO: "Call me—on the line!/You can call me, call me anytime!"

HOT DOGS

153

Let's Make a Doggy Sandwich

From: dam444
Sent: Friday, July 15, 2005 @ 4:43 PM
To: P/CAD
Subject: RE: Let's Make a Doggy Sandwich

WHAT I'M LOOKING FOR: PAD seeks P/CAD for romance and snack time companionship. Dams who get turned on by food are what I need. You love to eat before, during, and after sex.

WHY YOU WANT TO GET TO KNOW ME: I'm into the erotic aspects of food (yes, bread can be erotic—curious?) and I can shuck oysters as fast as any joker with opposable thumbs. My ability to obtain food from my humans is unrivaled in my neighborhood.

WHAT I'M WATCHING: *Babette's Feast, Like Water for Chocolate, Tampopo.*

MY FAVORITE PHYSICAL ACTIVITIES: Anything that involves working up a sweat AND chocolate sauce.

MY MOTTO: Live to eat, not eat to live.

Love Life Becalmed?

WHAT I'M LOOKING FOR: Newfoundland lobster dog seeks her very own personal selkie. You're a salty sea dog, as at home on the waves as you are curled on a couch on dry land.

WHY YOU WANT TO GET TO KNOW ME: I'm a PAD mariner who's been afloat most of my life. I'm first mate and dog captain of a small fishing boat, and have an easygoing, take-life-as-I-find-it attitude about life. Let's navigate the seas together.

MY PERFECT DATE: We'd meet at the docks. While the human got the boat underway, we would make sure everything was ship-shape. After an afternoon's fishing we'd head home to share a big bowl of fish chowder and then, who knows, perhaps compose a romantic sea-shanty about a couple of ocean-faring dogs in love.

WHAT I'M BEGGING FOR: Fish, raw or cooked. It's great for your coat and nails.

MY MOTTO: Wishing for fishes and fishing for wishes.

HOT DOGS
155

Help Me Out of the Closet

WHAT I'M LOOKING FOR: A caring PAD who loves PADs. I haven't been with another dam yet, so patience and understanding is a must. I'm not ready to tell my family yet, so discretion is important, too.

WHY YOU WANT TO GET TO KNOW ME: I'm a lover, not a fighter, and that's tough on a fighting breed. Personally, I just want to go through life taking time to sniff the flowers. I'm athletic and shy, with a big laugh.

PET PEEVES: Sure, there are occasions when a dog has to flex her shoulders, but I'm tired of little dogs with attitudes calling me out. Does Lassie have to choke a bitch every time?

WHAT'S IN MY BEDROOM: Weights, my iPod, Sleater-Kinney and Le Tigre posters, lilies in a vase.

MY MOTTO: Strong but silent wins the fight.

Sexy Mama!

Busy Little Bee

What I'm Looking For: You're a luscious flower, patiently waiting for my visit. Like me, you're a CAD interested in sucking deeply of life's heavenly nectars. Let's soar on warm currents of love, and when the mood strikes us, go back to the hive and buzz, buzz, buzz.

Why You Want To Get To Know Me: I'm the nurturing spirit of spring, spreading life from flower to flower. I dart hither and yon on my flickering wings. You share my sense of the ethereal and the transcendent. And you like the poetry of Edna St. Vincent Millay.

My Favorite Term of Endearment: Honey.

My Favorite Time of Year: May: Flowers are in bloom, birds are on the wing.

My Motto: Where the bee sucks, there suck I.

HOT DOGS
157

Lagoon Creature

From: dam10007
Sent: Thursday, Ju;y 7, 2005 @ 7:03 PM
To: CWD
Subject: RE: Lagoon Creature

WHAT I'M LOOKING FOR: Fellow CWD water freak, Loch Ness monster, or other aquatic eccentrics with whom to spend some quality time. Let's see if we can scare the locals, and take it from there.

WHY YOU WANT TO GET TO KNOW ME: I've been terrorizing a small lakeside community for some months now, and need to be taken in hand. Despite my fearsome looks, I'm a warm-hearted, assertive Pisces with a keen sense of humor. Just add water, though, and I'll make your skin crawl.

WHAT I'M WATCHING: Creature from the Black Lagoon, Plan 9 from Outer Space, Them, Splash!

WHAT'S IN MY BATHROOM: Seaweed scrub, flea bath, salt-mud facial, frightened townsfolk looking in through the window.

MY MOTTO: It lives!

HOT DOGS
158

DRIBBLING TOWARD LOVE

WHAT I'M LOOKING FOR: Either a strong defensive player or a versatile mid-fielder, all breeds welcome. No whiners, no quitters, please.

WHY YOU WANT TO GET TO KNOW ME: I'm a jock CAD extraordinaire, capable of playing a 90-minute soccer game without even breathing hard. I'm a fan, too, although I've been known to get overexcited and attack the opposing team's goalie. Needless to say, I'm intensely loyal.

WHERE I'D LIKE TO BE RIGHT NOW: Taking a shower with you after 90-plus minutes (extra periods are sooo sexy) of exhausting soccer.

WHAT'S IN MY BEDROOM: Soccer cleats (for chewing), signed Brandi Chastain poster, and a varsity sweater that belonged to the first Labrador I ever loved.

MY MOTTO: Play rough, but play fair and you'll never get a red card.

Calling All Linguists!

WHAT I'M LOOKING FOR: This PAD is looking for one thing and one thing only, ladies. If you know that tongues were made for more than talking, we've got something to discuss.

WHY YOU WANT TO GET TO KNOW ME: I'm a fun-loving, college-educated PAD (Smithies rule!) who likes to pamper herself. I like to pamper my friends, too: when you're part of my world, nothing's more important than feeling good. And when it comes to feeling good, I'm relentless.

MY PERFECT DAY: Long and lazy, lounging in the sun and lapping up each other's love.

WHAT'S IN MY BEDROOM: Manure-scented candles; beef-, pork-, and lamb-flavored erotic massage oils; *Bitch, Bitch, Bitch: Best Erotic Lesbian Fiction 2004*.

MY MOTTO: This tongue was made for walkin'/And that's just what it'll do/One of these days, this tongue/Is gonna walk all over you!

Like a Fresh Mountain Spring

From: dam614
Sent: Tuesday, July 26, 2005 @ 9:15 AM
To: CWD
Subject: RE: Like a Fresh Mountain Spring

WHAT I'M LOOKING FOR: The moment when the world stops and you realize you're in love. All I ask is that you are a romantic CWD who also believes that this is possible.

WHY YOU WANT TO GET TO KNOW ME: I'm an outdoorsy PAD, into hiking, camping, and foraging for wild foods. And, yes, I have a romantic side.

I'M MOST NEUROTIC ABOUT: I know they're semi-sentient animals in their own right, but I have a hard time believing that my humans will make it through the day on their own. I tend to be a bit of a "paws-on" dog, barking advice at them when they do things like drive a car or "communicate" with other humans.

MY DREAM VACATION: A week spent backpacking in the White Mountains of New Hampshire. Good paths and no ticks.

MY MOTTO: Hike in, hike out.

HOT DOGS
161

Brown-Eyed Poetess

WHAT I'M LOOKING FOR: A breathtakingly beautiful PWD who can leave me tongue-tied and helpless, or leave me wanting more—just never, ever leave me alone.

WHY YOU WANT TO GET TO KNOW ME: Isn't "high-strung" just another word for an artistic soul? Humans sometimes don't understand. Let's get together and go for long walks in thunderstorms, hang out with the bad dogs at the junkyard, and sit outside on a warm summer night and talk about the moon.

WHAT I'M READING: Anything by Gertrude Stein, Sylvia Plath, or T.S. Eliot (except *Old Possum's Book of Practical Cats*—what a crock!).

MY GREATEST AMBITION: To give a reading of my poetry at the dog run. In my vision, I start barking verses and every dog, human, and small rodent freezes in their tracks to soak up the beauty.

MY MOTTO: A dog is a dog is a dog is a dog.

Ooo La La!

HOT DOGS

Not Again!

What I'm Looking For:
A cynical C/PAD after my own heart, who takes the human folderol and festive hoo-hah with a pinch of flea powder. What I don't need is an overeager spaniel-type telling me to "just have a good time every now and then" (you know who you are). If your idea of fun is sitting in the corner making sarcastic comments, and generally taking a dim view of things, we should talk.

Why You Want To Get To Know Me: I am an intellectually burnt-out, post-grad PAD. Am I attractive? Only on the outside, honey, only on the outside....

Where I'd Like To Be Right Now: Luxuriating in a big vat of airplane glue. Anything beats Christmas.

What I Want For Christmas: What? Look, for the most part you can keep that stuff. Hand-knit hats, scarves, meat-flavored candy—feh. I could do some damage with professional-grade electronic surveillance equipment, but who would trust me with that?

My Motto: Bah, humbug!

HOT DOGS
163

From My Lips to Yours

From: dam303
Sent: Monday, July 25, 2005 @ 10:00 PM
To: PWD
Subject: RE: From My Lips to Yours

WHAT I'M LOOKING FOR:
A companion whose affection is commensurate with my own. I'm tired of loving, and giving, and getting nothing in return. You are a PWD with love in her heart and a smile on her lips!

WHY YOU WANT TO GET TO KNOW ME: This adoring, frisky terrier wants to plant a great big wet one on you. My boundless affection is contagious (but that's the only thing—I've had my shots). Plus, I can jump 6 feet in the air from a standing position.

MY BIGGEST FLAW: I tend to rush into relationships, and frighten off my dates by being too into them too soon. I wear my heart on my fur. Some call me needy, but I don't think I can change.

WORDS I'M DYING TO HEAR: "Would you like to go for a walk?"

MY MOTTO: Loving not wisely, but too well.

HOT DOGS
164

HANDY DAM

WHAT I'M LOOKING FOR: Little PAD seeks big-dog dam who could use a Ms. Fix-It-type for her home and her heart.

WHY YOU WANT TO GET TO KNOW ME: I'm extremely handy around the house, in more ways than one. And being of modest dimensions, I don't take up much space. Why don't we build a life together?

BEST THING I'VE BUILT: Call it a human baffle. I created a series of sliding panels that restrict my humans to one or two rooms in the house. They don't seem to notice the difference and get all the exercise they need in that space without wrecking the rest of the apartment.

WHAT I DO FOR FUN: I have an extensive small-pebble collection, and am active in the canine pebble-collecting community. Some of my best pebbles have been featured in *Drop That! The Monthly Newsletter of the Pebble Collecting Canines of America*.

MY MOTTO: Can do.

HOT DOGS
165

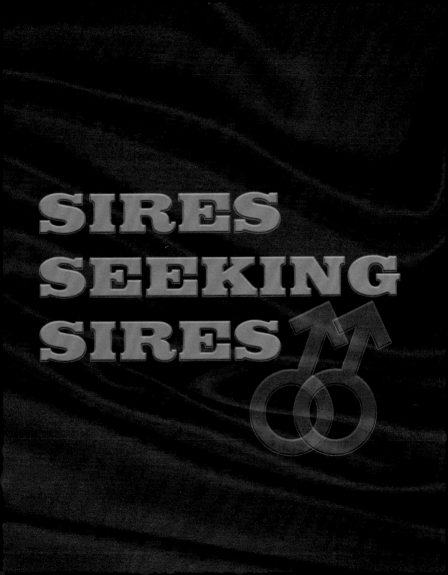

Gentlemen's Gentleman

WHAT I'M LOOKING FOR: Submissive PAS seeks position as love slave. I'm looking for a masterful dom dog, who wants to be waited on hand and foot. Mastiffs preferred.

WHY YOU WANT TO GET TO KNOW ME: I'm a very obedient PAS who will bring you your pipe and slippers when you get home, and wake you up with an invigorating tongue bath in the morning. I'll be your valet, your houseboy, your gardener, and your dog toy all rolled into one.

WHAT I'M WATCHING: *Jeeves and Wooster, My Man Godfrey, Mr. Belvedere.*

WHAT'S IN MY BED-ROOM: A pair of neatly shined, unchewed shoes, a white towel, a dog bed you can bounce a dime on.

MY MOTTO: Right away, sir!

Call Tonight!

HOT DOGS
168

A Little Bird Told Me

What I'm Looking For: Rochester, my avian buddy, tells me that it's high time I give up the life of a carefree bachelor and settle down with a nice sire. On this one subject I have decided to take his advice. You are a small PAS, with a sense of humor and a slim torso.

Why You Want To Get To Know Me: I'm a witty and good-natured dog of middle years, with an interest in the history of 18th-century pirates and privateers.

What I'm Reading: Treasure Island, Peter Pan, Captain Blood.

If I Wasn't A Dog I'd Like To Be: A parrot, sitting on the shoulder of a pirate who's screaming "splice the mainbrace" and "pieces of eight!"

My Motto: "Yo, ho, ho and a nice firm bum!"

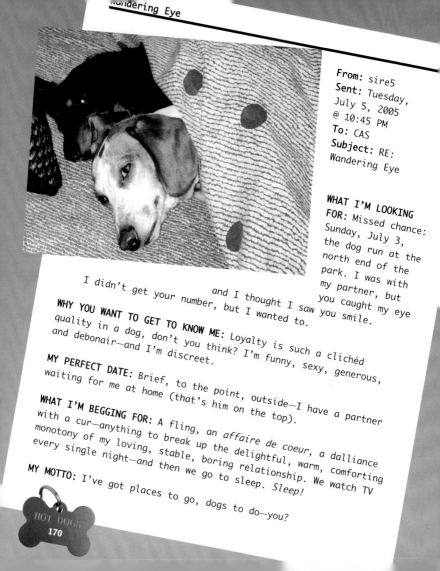

From: sire5
Sent: Tuesday, July 5, 2005 @ 10:45 PM
To: CAS
Subject: RE: Wandering Eye

WHAT I'M LOOKING FOR: Missed chance: Sunday, July 3, the dog run at the north end of the park. I was with my partner, but you caught my eye and I thought I saw you smile. I didn't get your number, but I wanted to.

WHY YOU WANT TO GET TO KNOW ME: Loyalty is such a clichéd quality in a dog, don't you think? I'm funny, sexy, generous, and debonair—and I'm discreet.

MY PERFECT DATE: Brief, to the point, outside—I have a partner waiting for me at home (that's him on the top).

WHAT I'M BEGGING FOR: A fling, an affaire de coeur, a dalliance with a cur—anything to break up the delightful, warm, comforting monotony of my loving, stable, boring relationship. We watch TV every single night—and then we go to sleep. *Sleep!*

MY MOTTO: I've got places to go, dogs to do—you?

HOT DOGS
170

PERSONAL
DESPERATE HOUSEPETS DATING SERVICE

FOOD CRITIC

WHAT I'M LOOKING FOR: You are a well-rounded CWS with great attention to detail. You're neat, can eat without calling attention to yourself, and are interested in the increasingly wide variety of foods available to the American canine. No Scorpios, please.

WHY YOU WANT TO GET TO KNOW ME: As part of my job as food critic for *Le Chowhound* magazine, I eat in literally hundreds of places a year, from my neighbor's trash can to top-notch international restaurants. I am a single CAS with considerable influence: my reviews reach an audience of thousands of dogs.

WHAT I'M WATCHING: The Food Channel's *Emeril Live*, *Iron Chef*, and *Molto Mario* are all favorites.

WHAT I'M BEGGING FOR: A carpaccio of foie gras with an anchovy veneer, the perfect pear.

MY MOTTO: With great power comes great responsibility—and meals on the house!

Curious George

WHAT I'M LOOKING FOR I'm looking for an experienced older dog for an afternoon rendezvous. How about my house? I'm not looking for a lifetime commitment, just an afternoon of experimentation—if there's chemistry, I guess anything could happen.

WHY YOU WANT TO GET TO KNOW ME: I'm a good-looking, bi-curious, big-boned PWS who's been dating dams since I was a sprightly 1-year-old, but I've often wondered what it would be like to be with another sire. Plus, I have a pool.

WHAT I'M BEGGING FOR: Tiny cheese cubes. Call me *le chien qui rit!*

MY FAVORITE PHYSICAL ACTIVITY: Sidewalk slalom: two dogs run, off-leash, through a forest of human legs along a stretch of sidewalk. Ready? Set. Go!

MY MOTTO: On the journey of life, new experiences are the mile-markers—I say, "rack 'em up!"

Hottie!

Bedroom Eyes

What I'm Looking For: Elegant ebony PAS seeks buff, neat sire with dark brown eyes and a sexy snout for lifting partner, possibly more. Non-shedders preferred.

Why You Want To Get To Know Me: I'm in top physical condition (I go to the dog run five days a week), but I'm tired of the same old faces and their tired old stories. I'm funny, I cook like a dream, and I'm ready to get serious.

I'm Most Neurotic About: Doors slamming in the distance. Can't people learn to open and close doors quietly? Weren't pneumatic hinges invented to prevent this nerve-rattling problem?

What's In My Bedroom: My bedroom is minimalist and elegant, with white linen, white walls, and white carpeting. Of course I'm always on the lookout for stray dog hairs.

My Motto: Let me hear your pillow talk and I'll rustle my sheets for you.

Be My Horse

From: sire939
Sent: Friday, April 29, 2005 @ 1:25 AM
To: PAS
Subject: RE: Be My Horse

WHAT I'M LOOKING FOR: Lean and muscular, slow-talking, prairie-grass chompin' PAS with immaculate style. You: Wear Italian cowboy boots, if you dare (I just might chew them right off your feet). Also, you're willing to dress up as livestock. No weirdos, please.

WHY YOU WANT TO GET TO KNOW ME: I'm all cowboy, in search of a stallion to ride. My range-riding is pretty much restricted to walking in the park, but the glimpses I've caught of cows and sheep at the petting zoo have convinced me that I'm in love with life on the ranch.

WHAT I'M WATCHING: Rhinestone Cowboy, McCloud, Urban Cowboy, ESPN's coverage of Xtreme Bulls, the bull-riding tour of the Professional Rodeo Cowboys Association (PRCA).

MY HOBBIES INCLUDE: Line dancing, herding mechanical cows, chasing electric sheep, riding bareback.

MY MOTTO: Hi-ho, Silver, away!

HOT DOGS
174

THE LITTLE DOG LAUGHED!

WHAT I'M LOOKING FOR: Why do the dish and spoon get to have all the fun? Little PWS seeks same, for good times, laughs, and, initially at least, a relationship that is not based on getting furry together.

WHY YOU WANT TO GET TO KNOW ME: I'm a fit, meth-free PWS, looking for a serious relationship that isn't based entirely on sex (been there, done that). Too often I feel that I'm on the outside of life, looking in. I hope you're willing to spend some time opening doors with a funny and creative dog like me.

I'M MOST NEUROTIC ABOUT: Animatronics. I can't pass one of those coin-operated ducks in the street without getting a little nervous. And I will never go to the Mohegan Sun Casino, where I understand they have animatronic wolves. Creepy!

IF I WASN'T A DOG I'D LIKE TO BE: A sleek, athletic ocelot. I know they're a form of cat—but they are slinky and cool and I don't get hung up on species.

MY MOTTO: Laughter is the best medicine, and the doctor is IN.

HOT DOGS
175

Serving Papers

WHAT I'M LOOKING FOR: A lover, a friend, and a lot more adventure in my life. You're a PS with a commanding presence, a visionary who can see the wood for the trees.

WHY YOU WANT TO GET TO KNOW ME: I'm a warm-hearted CAS and a devoted helpmeet for my humans, serving them as part-time clerk, gofer, and Johnny-on-the-spot. (They don't know I'm an amazing filer, and I'm in no rush to tell them.) Also, I love cars: front seat, back seat, behind the wheel—I always feel at home in an automobile!

WHAT I'M WATCHING: *9 to 5, Office Space, Working Girl.*

WHAT'S IN MY BEDROOM: *Dog Fancier,* arranged in chronological order, a small desk, and an absolutely tiny dog bed. I'm not expected to have guests, but it's time I had some help around here in the "office."

MY MOTTO: Gentlemen, start your search engines.

Call Tonight!

HOT DOGS
176

Park Fanatic

What I'm Looking For:
Dog-run veteran seeks friend to
cruise with. You: A well-muscled,
large breed with spiked collar and
a bad attitude (but you're smart,
clean, and well groomed, and
your mom loves you). No meth-
heads and no party boys, thanks.

**Why You Want To Get To
Know Me:** I'm a long-limbed,
athletic CWS with a good job
and a lot of room in my life for
a companion. I've made lots
of acquaintances at the dog
run, but it would be nice to
have a life partner with whom
to discuss the day's activities,
over drinks.

Pet Peeves: When hordes of
puppies and their moms take
over the dog run—if I ran
the thing, there would be
scheduled times for adults.

What I'm Begging For: Swiss cheese on a slice of still-warm baguette.

My Motto: You gotta have park (unless, of course, you live
in the countryside).

Rag Doll Chanteuse

From: sire69
Sent: Sunday, July 31, 2005 @ 7:56 PM
To: CWS
Subject: RE: Rag Doll Chanteuse

WHAT I'M LOOKING FOR: Torch-song diva looking for devoted younger fan. You are a doting CWS who'll come and see me perform and swan me around town afterwards. A lot of artistes don't have time for stage-door Johnnies, but I am very generous, as you'll see.

WHY YOU WANT TO GET TO KNOW ME: I'm a tenth-generation, purebred performer who's got greasepaint and showdogship in his blood. And when I put on my wig and sequined gown, sister, look out! I'm a fire-breathing cross between Judy Garland and Raggedy Ann.

WHAT I'M WATCHING: Victor/Victoria, The Adventures of Priscilla, Queen of the Desert, Outrageous, Nip/Tuck.

WHAT'S IN MY BEDROOM: One pair of purple Maude Frisson shoes, a Vera Wang bridesmaid dress from 1993, Best Damn Drag Dog (2003) trophy from Wigstock.

MY MOTTO: I'm more minx than harlot, and my bark is far worse than my bite (unless you go for that sort of thing, darling, in which case, make it a double vice versa on the rocks!).

HOT DOG!
178

P E R S O N A L
DESPERATE HOUSEPETS DATING SERVICE

I AM DIABLO, KING OF THE NIGHT!

WHAT I'M LOOKING FOR:
Innocent younger PWS, ripe for sweet corruption. Virgins preferred.

WHY YOU WANT TO GET TO KNOW ME:
I am an ancient soul, one of the original angels of pleasure, fallen to earth to spread the gospel. Let me introduce you to the world of devilish delights.

Together we'll revel in the sensual world, inspired by our lust for life and for living. Plus, I live in a great apartment with a view of the harbor.

WHAT I'M READING: *Dante's Inferno, The Devil's Dictionary, The Illustrated Kama Sutra* (the classics never go out of style).

WHAT'S IN MY (BASEMENT) BEDROOM: Animal skulls, erotic tapestries, an electric piano, and photographs of me in high school ("Most Likely to Run Away and Join the Circus").

MY MOTTO: It's your thing—do whatcha wanna do.

Mountain Goat

WHAT I'M LOOKING FOR: You're in touch with your spiritual side; you have a good sense of humor, but know when to take things seriously. You are an outdoorsy PWS interested in living in harmony with the natural world.

WHY YOU WANT TO GET TO KNOW ME: People tell me I'm not like other Aries. I'm a peacemaker, creative, and I'm an excellent mediator. My first lover was part coyote, and I learned a lot from him about the cycles of the moon, chasing smaller creatures, and digging holes.

MY FAVORITE BEVERAGES: The essence of morning in the mountains: Dew on a shiny leaf. Also, Colorado River water and lime-flavored Gatorade.

MY GREATEST AMBITION: To walk on the wild side/run with a wolf pack.

MY MOTTO: Do you get that Rocky Mountain High when the shadow from the starlight is softer than a lullaby? Me, too.

From: sire5091
Sent: Friday, July 1, 2005
@ 10:14 AM
To: PWS
Subject: RE: International
Scenester

WHAT I'M LOOKING FOR:
Versatile party pooch
whose tastes run
the gamut from night-
clubs to warehouse
parties to open-air,
all-night raves. You
are young, hot, and too much
is never enough for you. Must have
valid passport.

WHY YOU WANT TO GET TO KNOW ME: This PAS works as an international DJ, so I travel a lot. I have a lot of friends, but I
can be a little caustic, so it's critical that you appreciate
my wit (okay, fear my wit). If you're good, though, we'll go
all night, every night—I happen to know a "pharmacy" that's
always open.

MY FAVORITE OUTFIT: Evil Pink Troll (that's me in a rave in a
loft in Belfast, 2002).

WHAT'S IN MY BEDROOM: A pile of newspapers, discarded wrist-
bands, pacifiers, candy necklaces, empty water bottles. Who
has time to sleep?

MY MOTTO: Pretty in pink.

HOT DOGS
181

Oscar Seeks Felix

WHAT I'M LOOKING FOR: A neatnik, house-proud, finicky fool, who'll take pity on me and do a few dishes around here. You're a slim, handsome PAS, and better than I deserve.

WHY YOU WANT TO GET TO KNOW ME: Honesty's all I know. I'm a slob, but I know I'm a slob, and what I lack in panache I more than make up for in playful affection. I don't think anybody needs a hug, but somebody around here definitely needs a big slobbery kiss. Pucker up!

WHAT I'M WATCHING: Anything by Neil Simon, *Cops*, USTA events.

Ooo La La!

WHAT'S IN MY BEDROOM: Flea collars (lots and lots of flea collars), used doggy bags, other people's dirty laundry.

MY MOTTO: If I'm using it again tomorrow, why is it, exactly, that I can't just drop it here on the floor where I won't miss it on my way out in the morning?

Lap Dog

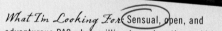

What I'm Looking For: Sensual, open, and adventurous PAS who's willing to explore the world in a tactile way. Despite your powerful sense of smell, you are not fazed by the words "dog breath."

Why You Want To Get To Know Me: I'm a versatile linguist, who can bark in English and French, and speak three out of five Peke dialects. I'm an avid golfer and I excel at pocket pool.

My Heroes: Chameleons, Gene Simmons.

What's In My Medicine Chest: Listerine pocket-packs, Scope, Oralpal mint dog bones.

My Motto: A dog in the lap is better than two in the bush.

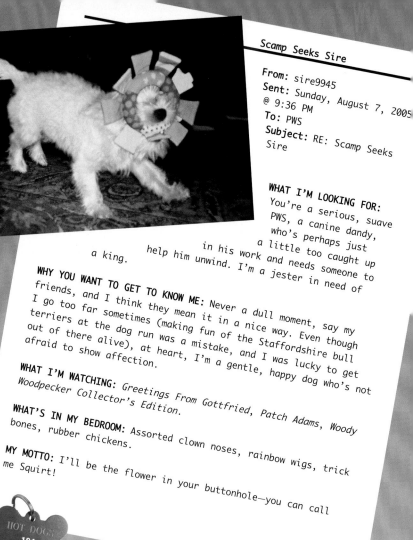

Scamp Seeks Sire

From: sire9945
Sent: Sunday, August 7, 2005 @ 9:36 PM
To: PWS
Subject: RE: Scamp Seeks Sire

WHAT I'M LOOKING FOR: You're a serious, suave PWS, a canine dandy, who's perhaps just a little too caught up in his work and needs someone to help him unwind. I'm a jester in need of a king.

WHY YOU WANT TO GET TO KNOW ME: Never a dull moment, say my friends, and I think they mean it in a nice way. Even though I go too far sometimes (making fun of the Staffordshire bull terriers at the dog run was a mistake, and I was lucky to get out of there alive), at heart, I'm a gentle, happy dog who's not afraid to show affection.

WHAT I'M WATCHING: *Greetings From Gottfried, Patch Adams, Woody Woodpecker Collector's Edition.*

WHAT'S IN MY BEDROOM: Assorted clown noses, rainbow wigs, trick bones, rubber chickens.

MY MOTTO: I'll be the flower in your buttonhole—you can call me Squirt!

PERSONALS

LIVING IN THE '80S

WHAT I'M LOOKING FOR: You are a with-it PWS with warm feelings about (but please, no actual memories of) the mousse decade. You have a love of peg pants, big hair, and pop-inflected melancholia that you can really dance to.

WHY YOU WANT TO GET TO KNOW ME: I never stopped thinking BIG and living every day as if it might be last. I've been through tough times (the grunge era was, shall we say, unkind), but I'm a resilient dog with the moxie to stand up for what I believe in. Let's meet, flick the hair out of our faces, and gaze into each other's eyes.

WHAT I'M LISTENING TO: Flock of Seagulls, New Order, The Smiths, Junior Senior.

WHAT'S IN MY BEDROOM: Neon-colored dog accessories, dark mascara, my industrial-size vat of hair gel, Zebra-striped dog bed.

MY MOTTO: "Don't you want me, baby?"

HOT DOG!
185

Back to Our Roots

WHAT I'M LOOKING FOR: Hungry CWS seeks ruggedly handsome CAS who shares my atavistic delight in the consumption of raw meat. You are not a finicky eater and the very thought of kibble sends you coughing and retching for the doggy door.

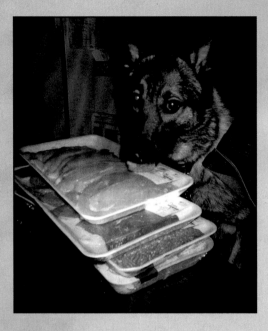

WHY YOU WANT TO GET TO KNOW ME: I'm a back-to-basics carnivore: no cereal fillers and no meat substitutes for me. Let's celebrate our essential canine nature with an epicurean feast liberated from the omnivorous humans' freezers. With me, you will always eat as our ancestors did (even if we're forced to carefully remove the plastic packing to avoid choking).

WHAT I'M WATCHING: The butcher's shop window.

WHAT'S IN MY BEDROOM: A poster from the U.S. Beef Council showing various cuts of steer, map of the migratory route of the American Bison, and a jumbo spool of dental floss.

MY MOTTO: Whether it's rock-hard muscle or throbbing gristle, it's probably something I'd like to devour.

Work Out

WHAT I'M LOOKING FOR: A PWS who's young, energetic, and in great physical shape for running partner, best friend (sorry, other best friend—the human comes first), and maybe more? You can always nip at my heels if I you think I'm getting out of control, but you'll have to catch me first!

WHY YOU WANT TO GET TO KNOW ME: I'm a sincere romantic with a great sense of humor—and I'm a triathlete (my swimming and running are great, but I'm still working on the digging part of my training regimen). I've tried picking up pooches at the gym, but it's so impersonal and everyone's at their most vain—get over yourselves!

WHAT I'M WATCHING: Tails of Steel exercise video, Keeping Fit: Friskiness in the Car, Dogs of GQ.

MY BIGGEST SECRET: I was the runt of the litter.

MY MOTTO: "Cry havoc and let loose the dogs!"

HOT DOGS
187

Are You The One?

WHAT I'M LOOKING FOR: Sensitive, submissive CAS seeks same for friendship, conversation, and more, possibly leading to long-term commitment. You clean up after yourself, never bark indoors, and share my love of collectible dolls. Short-hair breed a plus.

WHY YOU WANT TO GET TO KNOW ME: I may be a bit obsessive about cleanliness and order, but I'm an old-fashioned dog who's in touch with my feelings. My doll collection is my pride and joy; if you respect that about me, maybe we could set up house together.

MY THREE BIGGEST TURN-OFFS: Slobberers, aggressive, macho showoffs, and messy eaters.

WHAT'S IN MY BEDROOM: Color-coordinated sheets in tasteful floral patterns, original cast recording of *Cats*, my prized 14" Robert Tonner "Betsy McCall" (among others).

MY MOTTO: No, no, no, I insist—after you.

Hottie!

HOT DOGS

188

Rudolph Seeks Blitzen

What I'm Looking For: Santa's little helper. You're a tiny PWS on the borderline between fairy and elf, with pointy features and that great small-dog enthusiasm and energy. Sorry, no yippers and no snappers.

Why You Want To Get To Know Me: I'm a jolly old PWS with a belly that shakes when I laugh, and an enthusiastic taste for hot erotic role-play. I'm a naturally giving "long-horned" beast, who wants someone to relish my ample attentions.

What I'm Watching: *Frosty the Snowman, The Grinch That Stole Christmas, A Charlie Brown Christmas,* and *Bend Over, Rover 3.*

My Greatest Achievement: Last year I managed to salvage my old dog-bed after my humans accidentally put it in the garbage. Imagine their joy as I dragged it to the table during Christmas dinner!

My Motto: Unlike Christmas, this reindeer comes more than once a year—a lot more!

HOT DOGS
189

Slightly Fearful

From: sire7791
Sent: Sunday, August 7, 2005 @ 3:34 PM
To: PAS
Subject: RE: Slightly Fearful

WHAT I'M LOOKING FOR: A sympathetic lover who'll join me under the covers. Together we'll create our own small world and shut out the larger one, careless and cruel as it is. You're a small-breed (there's only so much room under here) PAS who doesn't mind spending the day in bed. Disease-free, please.

WHY YOU WANT TO GET TO KNOW ME: Despite my timid nature, I have a vivid imagination and lead a rich and adventurous fantasy life. Benefits for you include a warm and comfortable setting for our romance, and good bedtime stories.

WHAT I'M READING: The Lord of the Rings, The Wind in the Willows, and The Erotic Adventures of Lord Gaydog (not all my fantasies are PG).

MY PERFECT DATE: You come over to my house. We curl up on the couch and check out some videos. Then, we recreate our favorite scenes between the sheets.

MY MOTTO: Baby, it's cold outside—but it's cozy and warm in here!

HOT DOGS
190

DISCIPLINE & PUNISH

WHAT I'M LOOKING FOR: I'm a very naughty little dog who has been breaking all the rules, and I need a strapping, large-breed guard to put me in my place—just not solitary confinement, please! You're a PWS top, who knows a thing or two about keeping disobedient pups like me in line.

WHY YOU WANT TO GET TO KNOW ME: I'm a hardened con, but I'm all dog. And while I'm very sorry about what I've done, I know "sorry" just doesn't cut it. I may need to have my yard privileges revoked.

MY PERFECT DATE: The prison is in lock down, but one prisoner is still mouthing off to the guards. It's time to teach him a lesson. You appear at the door of my cell....

WHAT'S IN MY BEDROOM: My Spartan cell contains nothing but top-of-the-line restraints and a large selection of perfectly balanced rolled-up newspapers designed for spankin' without leaving a mark. Also, a shock collar.

MY MOTTO: I've been a bad, bad boy.

HOT DOGS
191

Copilot Sought

WHAT I'M LOOKING FOR: Saint-Exupéry seeks Little Prince to be copilot for my journey to the stars. Some dogs are born with their feet cemented to the earth, but together you and I will soar. Let's get together for a test flight.

WHY YOU WANT TO GET TO KNOW ME: I've got nerves of steel and a poet's soul. With me at the controls you'll always fly first class, whether it's across the street, across the country, or all the way to the Dog Star and beyond.

WHAT I'M READING: *The Little Prince, Starship Troopers, Snoopy vs. the Red Baron, Laika: First Dog in Space.*

ALWAYS IN MY FLIGHT JACKET: A compass, a guide to the night sky, individual packets of Kibbles 'n Bits.

MY MOTTO: *Ad Astra per Aspera.*

HOT DOGS
192

Got Milk Duds?

From: sire1031
Sent: Friday, August 2, 2005 @ 11:49 AM
To: PAWS
Subject: RE: Got Milk Duds?

WHAT I'M LOOKING FOR: A sweetheart PA/WS to disprove the axiom that purebreds are cold-hearted snobs and make lousy lovers.

WHY YOU WANT TO GET TO KNOW ME: I'll do anything for candy, which makes me a cheap date. I'm a CAS myself, although BOTH my parents (so I know all about the scuttlebutt) were purebreds. I'm loving and trusting, despite my experience in the dating world.

MY FAVORITE CANDY: Mary Janes, lime jellybeans, horehound lozenges.

MY FAVORITE HOLIDAY: Halloween, obviously, but both Easter and Christmas have traditions that satisfy this dog's sweet tooth. I got in really big trouble once for chasing down the Easter Bunny. I thought I might be able to scare the livin' chocolate Easter eggs out of him....

MY MOTTO: Tough but sweet.

HOT DOGS
193

Sing a Song

What I'm Looking For:
Large-breed CAS with operatic
presence. It's not just about
howling at the moon, it's about the
way you move. Whether you perform
your best on stage dressed as the
Norse god Thor or you are a secret
shower-diva, I want to hear the
songs you're singing.

**Why You Want To Get To
~~Know~~ Me:** Large-voiced and
bighearted, I'm seldom without a
song on my lips. While humans
sometimes misunderstand my
art, my enthusiasm should
appeal to dogs.

What I'm Listening To: Montserrat
Caballé singing *Carmen*, Gilbert and Sullivan performed by the
D'Oyly Carte, *Der Ring des Nibelungen* performed at the Bayreuth Festival.

What I Do For Fun: I like to go to the opera house and sneak on stage
during the crowd scenes. Some of the productions are so busy, they don't notice
there isn't supposed to be a dog in the barbershops of Seville or on board the
H.M.S. Pinafore!

My Motto: Many lads have loved a sailor, so I consider myself in
good company!

Film Buff

WHAT I'M LOOKING FOR: Creative, honest, good-looking PAS, interested both in being and doing, well-adjusted, with an encyclopedic knowledge of film, from Georges Méliès to George Romero. Come in for an interview on my casting couch—if you've got the right stuff, maybe we can start by making some short films together.

WHY YOU WANT TO GET TO KNOW ME: I'm a video hound with a lot of love in my heart. I'm a straight-shooting, quietly sexy PAS who survived a darkly twisted puppyhood to become the dog I am today. I'm sort of a cross between *Dirty Harry*–era Clint and Marcello Mastroiani.

A SURPRISING FACT ABOUT ME: *Lady and the Tramp* is in my movie Top Ten.

WHAT I'M WATCHING: *Cujo* (of course), *The Dog Who Cried Wolf*, *The Hound of the Baskervilles*, *Intervista*.

MY MOTTO: Lights! Camera! Action!

Ooo La La!

Top Hat

From: sire10
Sent: Monday, August 1, 2005 @ 8:30 PM
To: PAS
Subject: RE: Top Hat

WHAT I'M LOOKING FOR: From the tip of your aristocratic nose to your neatly clipped toenails, you are a class act. You are a PAS more at home in evening clothes than your birthday suit. No photograph, no reply. And please, no whole sires: gentledogs get clipped.

WHY YOU WANT TO GET TO KNOW ME: I'm a really, really good dog, who dresses well and wants to be around other dogs of similarly sartorial bent. And I insist on the best of everything: I've had a number of relationships fail, after an initial attraction, because of a difference in breeding.

MY PERFECT DATE: We attend a gala affair, a benefit for the ASPCA. They serve really lovely canapés made with foie gras, but we only graze. Afterwards we go for cocktails at the Carlyle and dinner at the Plaza. Your place or mine?

WHAT'S IN MY BEDROOM: My bedroom is filled with lovely things, but best of all is a Chippendale dresser.

MY MOTTO: No more wire hangers.

HOT DOG!
196

P E R S O N A L S

DESPERATE HOUSEPETS DATING SERVICE

TOP DOG / UNDERDOG

WHAT I'M LOOKING FOR: Mature PAS seeks quiet, large-breed PAS, with an interest in the arts, tennis balls, and antique woodworking.

WHY YOU WANT TO GET TO KNOW ME: I am a seasoned terrier who, despite my size, is a masterful alpha dog who handles subordinates with refreshing efficiency. No loud arguments, no quarrelsome barking. You'll know your place and you'll like it (the CAS in the photo didn't last too long—too uppity for his own good).

BEST CHILDHOOD EXPERIENCE: Realizing that we are NOT created equal. From the day I first opened my eyes it was clear to me that a) my mother loved me more than all of my brothers and sisters and b) I could have as much milk as I wanted.

WORST LIE I EVER TOLD: "Go ahead, you go first. I don't mind at all." Oh, wait—I never, ever said any such thing.

MY MOTTO: Power is the greatest aphrodisiac—make mine a double.

HOT DOGS
197

Basket Case

WHAT I'M LOOKING FOR: You are the calm at the center of my storm. You are a super-patient, indulgent PAS who can play Mr. Rogers to the frightened child within me.

WHY YOU WANT TO GET TO KNOW ME: I'm a shy CAS who has difficulty making new friends, but I'm quite sweet-natured and a good conversationalist once you get to know me. Help this erotic/neurotic flower.

I'M MOST NEUROTIC ABOUT: Being late for anything. It doesn't matter if it's a dental appointment or a gallery opening, I have to get there at least 10 minutes before the doors open or I have a complete meltdown. Also, dirty laundry.

WHAT'S IN MY BEDROOM: Worry beads, security blanket, doggy shrink on speed dial.

MY MOTTO: They're not irrational fears if they can actually, possibly happen.

Hot Chocolate and Cookies

From: sire2580
Sent: Friday, July 15, 2005 @ 4:35 PM
To: PWS
Subject: RE: Hot Chocolate and Cookies

WHAT I'M LOOKING FOR: An intelligent, well-put-together PWS, who has a taste for roasted chestnuts, running after snowballs, and jumping through fresh powder.

WHY YOU WANT TO GET TO KNOW ME: Summer is delightful, My spring divine, and very little beats a brisk fall day. My favorite time of year, however, is winter. The air is crisp and clean, and fresh snowfall has a way of returning a sense of innocence to the earth. Won't you join me on a winter's evening for an invigorating walk in the park and a quiet talk by the fire over cocoa and cookies?

PET PEEVE: Yellow snow. We're not savages, here, folks.

WHAT'S IN MY BEDROOM: Roaring fire, slippers, fine Kentucky bourbon.

MY MOTTO: Cold paws, warm heart.

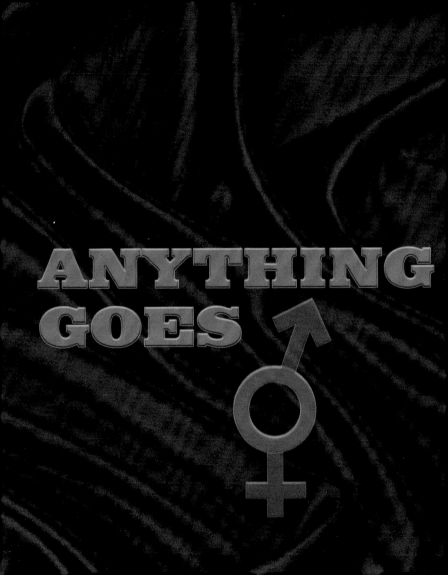

Dogpile

From: dogpile1
Sent: Tuesday,
August 9, 2005
@ 6:14 PM
To: PWS
Subject: RE:
Dogpile

WHAT WE'RE LOOKING FOR: Adventurous PWS sought to round out a dogpile quad. You are attitude- and disease-free. You've probably seen a dogpile, the traditional canine ceremony of sexual celebration, but possibly you've been afraid to join in. Now's your chance.

WHY YOU WANT TO GET TO KNOW US: We're a small, family-based pack of 3 very intelligent, very enlightened beagles who will lead you through the sensual process of self-discovery and erotic growth that group sex can bring. Also, we're superb cooks.

A SURPRISING FACT ABOUT US: Our multimillion-bone catering business started when we were forced to retire from our traditional job of chasing foxes. Necessity, as it turns out, is the mother of reinvention.

WHAT'S IN OUR BEDROOM: The first thing you'll notice is the sense of peace that envelopes you as you enter. Canine feng shui experts have been consulted to create an atmosphere of absolute trust (plus there's a faint scent of raw liver in the air), in which to best experience the traditional dogpile process.

OUR MOTTO: There's always room for one more.

HOT DOGS
202

PACK SEEKS LEADER

WHAT WE'RE LOOKING FOR: Mixed pack seeks P/CA/WS/D. You're an alpha dog, a real decision maker, a hound who knows when to chase cats, when to chill out, and when to snuffle around in garbage. We need you to be

our leader—we spent last weekend nipping at each other's heels instead of looking for something dead to roll in. Loud, full-throated howl a plus.

WHY YOU WANT TO GET TO KNOW US: We've got the skills, we just need a CEO to transform us from a collection of random pooches into a pack with purpose. Also, how often in life do you get the opportunity to shoot to the top of the ladder without having to sweat the details and tedium of putting together a team from scratch?

WHAT WE'RE WATCHING: *Dances with Wolves*, *The Dirty Dozen*, *Easy Rider*, *Ocean's Eleven*.

OUR MOTTO: United we stand, divided we amble around aimlessly, trying to flesh out the bewilderingly empty moments of yet another leaderless day....

HOT DOGS

203

I'll Be Your Boy/Girl Toy

WHAT I'M LOOKING FOR: Stuffed animal seeks dog companion. Own teeth: not necessarily a plus. Gender and breed are not issues, as I possess no genitalia and was not born of dog. I have over the years been all things to many dogs.

WHY YOU WANT TO GET TO KNOW ME: I'm coming out of a long-term relationship (that's my ex on the right), and I have some healing to do. Let's take things slowly and get to know each other. I'm a good listener and very submissive — there will be no fights over dog-bowl access in our relationship!

WORST LIE I EVER TOLD: "It's not you: I'm just not into dogs right now."

WHAT'S IN MY BEDROOM: All the stuff that's in your bedroom. Plus me.

MY MOTTO: Once you go stuffed, you can't get enough.

Blofeld Seeks Adjutant

From: cws66666
Sent: Friday, August 12, 2005 @ 7:12 PM
To: CAD
Subject: RE: Blofeld Seeks Adjutant

WHAT I'M LOOKING FOR: You're a CAD born to be second-in-command, able to carry out my orders without a moment's hesitation. Must be entirely ruthless: sentiment is a weakness, all must obey. Among your duties will be light cleaning and being my sexual plaything.

WHY YOU WANT TO GET TO KNOW ME: I am a brilliant and ruthless, if tiny, CWS. The world needs a ruler like me, and if it doesn't know that now, it will soon. I can already control my human using only my mind; think of what could be ours under my leadership!

IF I RULED THE WORLD: I would abolish vets everywhere and submit humans to selective sterilization (to prevent overbreeding—they're much happier that way). No more cute sweaters for little dogs!

WORST LIE I EVER TOLD: "Greater security demands that we give up some of our personal liberties."

MY MOTTO: Slavery is freedom.

HOT DOGS
205

Fight Club Members Wanted

WHAT I'M LOOKING FOR: You think you're a tough dog, but actually you're a wuss, a house pet, a lapdog, a poodle, a half-weaned puppy, paper-trained, and choke-chained. You're nothing but a pretty, little, bitty, kitty cat. Think I'm wrong? Come tell me to my face.

WHY YOU WANT TO GET TO KNOW ME: I'm the meanest, baddest, strongest, best-looking PWS you'll ever meet. And that's my hydrant you're sidling up to. You want to know me 'cause you want to find out why and how I own you. Bitch.

WHAT I'M EATING: Gravel, armchairs, you—for dinner.

WHAT'S IN MY BEDROOM: Chewed-up boxing gloves, poster from *Rocky III* (The Greatest Challenge!), picture of mom.

MY MOTTO: Cats run away and humans have to use pepper spray, but dogs stand and fight.

Paradise Club Seeks Clients

What I'm Looking For: Discerning callers, dams or sires, who want only the best and don't mind paying for it. The talented ladies of the Widdle School of Sensuous Massage are ready to service you. Every ending a happy one.

Why You Want To Get To Know Us: Our agency provides escorts to dog shows, quiet dinners, or comfortable evenings at home. Or you can come visit our comfortable kennels. "Special services" available price to be determined—no request too outlandish.

What We're Watching: The Duchess of Duke Street, The Best Little Whorehouse in Texas, Pretty Baby, Spice channel.

What's In Our Bedrooms: Pack-size dog bed with Prada sheets, ceiling mirrors, full-service wet bar.

Our Motto: The customer is always right.

Looking for Baby Mama

From: sire5511
Sent: Monday, February 18, 2005 @ 6:11 AM
To: PWD
Subject: RE: Looking for Baby Mama

WHAT I'M LOOKING FOR: You are a dam of any breed, interested in being pregnant. You don't want someone to love, you're just looking for a donor.

WHY YOU WANT TO GET TO KNOW ME: I enjoy doing it doggy-style and impregnating dams of all breeds, but I get a special thrill from doing it with a purebred dam and leaving her with a litter of mutts. If you're looking to get back at your human, this could be the perfect way.

MY GREATEST AMBITION: To get it on with a Standard Poodle. Those snobs never give me the time of day, so I'd love to just stick it to one of 'em....

MOST EMBARASSING MOMENT: I once mounted a dog from behind and it turned out to be another sire! I may be into all breeds, but I only want dams, please.

MY MOTTO: Dip your paw in all the wells.

HOT DOGS
208

DESIGNING DOGS

WHAT WE'RE LOOKING FOR: Home and wardrobe design consulting team seeks clients. Hire us to transform your doghouse from a place of wearisome exile to an up-to-the-minute love nest.

WHY YOU WANT TO GET TO KNOW US: Design-maven brothers, trained in Europe with particular emphasis on Scandinavian interiors and Finnish fire hydrants. Who wouldn't want to know us?

OUR FAVORITE PIECE OF DESIGN: The leg bone of a Hereford steer (it's a meal with its own carrying handle), Alessi "Lupita" dog bowl, and the choke chain (for its devilish ingenuity: just how does it know you're about to run away?)

WHAT CATALOGS WE'RE GETTING: *Marimekko, Design Within Reach, Design of Denmark, Engelbrechts.*

OUR MOTTO: Less costs more.

Call Tonight!

HOT DOGS
209

Barky Boys Detective Agency

WHAT WE'RE LOOKING FOR: Jilted lovers, angry spouses, worried parents—come one, come all! Have you lost bones? Are you being watched by squirrels? Do you want to know what the postman is up to after he leaves your house, and why?

WHY YOU WANT TO GET TO KNOW US: We are snappy, spunky, sleuthy triplets who will hunt down the facts with a tenacity that belies our tender years, utilizing our innate curiosity and powerful sniffers.

WHAT WE'RE READING/WATCHING: *Hardy Boys*, *Nancy Drew*, *Scooby-Doo*.

OUR BIGGEST FLAW: Our enthusiasm sometimes causes us to lose focus. We were once on the trail of some missing shoelaces when a bag of last night's garbage passed by at puppy level so we followed it for leads, then all of a sudden we caught sight of our tails and—hey, what's that?!

OUR MOTTO: No clue undigested, no trash can lid unturned.

Double Trouble

From: Trouble_x2
Sent: Tuesday, June 23, 2005
@ 11:47 PM
To: PAS
Subject: RE: Double Trouble

WHAT WE'RE LOOKING FOR: The *ménage à trois* is, we feel, a very natural grouping for dogs. We're a PAS and a PAD seeking a small-breed sire to help us keep our hearth warm at night.

WHY YOU WANT TO GET TO KNOW US: We're a delightful, fun-loving couple (call us Nick and Nora), even if we drink heavily and have the habit of looking over each other's shoulders to see who just entered the room.

WHAT WE'RE WATCHING: *Jules et Jim, Cabaret, A Small Circle of Friends.*

OUR PERFECT DAY: Riding up and down in the elevator in our apartment building. It's a great place to people- and dog-watch (eventually, almost everybody in the world has to take the elevator), and catch up on gossip.

OUR MOTTO: Three really is company!

HOT DOG!
211

Strange Bedfellows

WHAT I'M LOOKING FOR: Sure, dogs chase cats. But what happens when they catch them? Are you the special someone we've been looking for? My feline partner and I are looking for the right dog. Are you open-minded enough to experiment with interspecies polyandry?

WHY YOU WANT TO GET TO KNOW ME: I'm a PAS who's learned a lot from my relationships with cats: the sex secrets of the ancient Egyptians, how to gut a mouse, how to purr. Getting together with us will take your love life to a higher plane.

WHAT I'M WATCHING: *Cat People*, *The Aristocats*, *Cats and Dogs*.

I'M MOST NEUROTIC ABOUT: Litter boxes. Those things still give me the heebie-jeebies.

MY MOTTO: Here kitty, kitty, kitty.

Chain of Fools

What We're Looking For: Another member, of either sex, for our troop of extraordinary erotic athletes. We believe in the transcendent power of canine sexuality. We perform at the peak of physical fitness, so you need to be in great shape, both physically and mentally.

Why You Want To Get To Know Us: We're hot little PADs, with coiled gymnast bodies. What we do serves a higher purpose, but it's also incredibly sexy. Just don't call it an orgy!

Pet Peeve: Humans think we're cute.

What's In Our Bedroom: Swing set, harnesses and trapeze equipment, leather-covered slide.

My Motto: Multum in parvo.

WHAT I'M LOOKING FOR: PWS seeks hairy, slightly feral human dam for exploration of interspecies relationship. You are friendly, don't wash too often, and are curious about what it might be like to date a dog. Must have all shots.

WHY YOU WANT TO GET TO KNOW ME: I'm a literate, compassionate housebound PWS, who has yet to find a meaningful romantic relationship with another dog. I'm constantly hearing the humans say, "He thinks he's a person" (that's me in the photo, opening a birthday present from my mother last year). I really like my humans, but on a strictly platonic level—I'm not sure, but I feel there could be something more with the right person... maybe you?

MY PERFECT DATE: You pick me up at my house and take me to the beach, where we play in the surf and scamper across the sand all day. As the families start packing up and heading home, we retire to the dunes to watch the sun set. I roll over. You scratch my belly and my leg begins to twitch. Our eyes meet....

I'M MOST NEUROTIC ABOUT: What will our friends say?

MY MOTTO: Human, all too human.

HOT DOGS
214

WHAT A PIECE OF WORK IS DOG

WHAT I'M LOOKING FOR: Energetic PAD seeks thespians of every description to join revolutionary new troupe of actors devoted to performing the Bard's works for canine audiences throughout North America. Dogs only, please!

WHY YOU WANT TO GET TO KNOW ME:
I'm a literate, committed performer with a long list of stage successes on her résumé, both On and Off-Broadway, as well as in several touring companies (my longest stint was with the Dallas Rep). I won the Tallulah Doghead Circle in the Square audience award for Best Dog in Show (1999) for my performance as Crab in *Two Gentleman of Verona*, which got me to thinking: Why not start an all-dog Shakespearean company? Will did it without women, and I felt I could do it without any people whatsoever. The NEH agreed, and now the hunt for talent is on!

MY TURN-OFFS: Insincerity, bad line readings, prima donnas, critics.

MY MOTTO: All the world's a stage, and all the sires and dams merely players....

Sorcerer's Apprentice

WHAT I'M LOOKING FOR: A magical mentor. You're a talented older magician PA/WS and alchemist, capable of turning base metal into dog bones (and reversing this horrid spell that has given me mouse ears).

WHY YOU WANT TO GET TO KNOW ME: I am a gifted amateur magic-wielder, but I am untutored. So, while I'm not afraid to dabble in the dark arts, my efforts are frequently misdirected (hence, the accidental addition of rodent ears—how embarrassing!). This PWS would welcome a close personal bond with a more experienced magical practitioner. Plus, I'll scrub your broomstick, if you like.

WHAT'S IN MY BEDROOM: Crystal balls, base metals, very few bones.

WHAT I'M BEGGING FOR: Eye of newt on a dog biscuit—hold the powdered batwing, please!

MY MOTTO: Abracadabra!

Call Tonight!

Claw Me Up Sometime

From: sire23
Sent: Thursday,
August 4, 2005
@ 2:30 AM
To: C/PA/WD
Subject: RE: Claw
Me Up Sometime

WHAT I'M LOOKING FOR: You're a female cat with all her claws who's interested in experiencing a little dog love. I'll pretend to chase you and you'll claw back with all your might, then we'll wrestle and overturn furniture, until I finally overtake you and teach you how we do it in the dog pound.

WHY YOU WANT TO GET TO KNOW ME: I'm a CWS who enjoys the "hunt," and I love felines. I discovered my attraction when a hot white Persian clawed my nose and then began to lick me all over with her rough little tongue.

MY GREATEST AMBITION: I want to make you say, "meow," over and over, and then make you say it some more.

MOST EMBARRASSING MOMENT: I tried to mount an Egyptian Mau and her owner pulled me off mid-thrust.

MY MOTTO: What's up, pussy cat?

HOT DOG!
217

Index of Dog Owners

Photography Credits, by Page Number

61: Livingstone, Holly (Mohave)
62: Cartabio, Emilio (Sir Chadwick Diamond Star)
63: Leonard, Ana (Paco)
64: Antoniades, Deb (Daisy)
65: Schultz, Ronnie
66: Shank, Erin (Sadie)
67: Kingsley, Nathaniel (Libby)
68: Weiss, Linda (Casey)
69: Greig, June (Bailey)
70: Meuller, Jan (Missy)
71: Bogues, Keith and Nancy (Stryder)
72: Wolling, Jessica (Nicky)
73: Beedle, Kim (Ginger)
74: O'Nan-Johnson, Lucy (Tucker)
75: Duthie, Ken and Maria (Flip)
76: Mifsud, Therese (Sadie)
77: Faircloth, Jane/Transparencies, Inc. (Jessie)
78: McGoey, Teresa (Tucker, Diesel)
79: Marchese, Melissa (Bijou)
80: Jacobson, Rachel (Sammy)
81: Zayats, Yelena (Franky)
82: Larsen, Virginia (Kelly)
83: Sorrell, Wendy (Chaz)
84: Poe, Andrea (Sherman "Tank" Poe)
85: Mifsud, Therese (Champ)
86: Rosen-Zohar, Lily/Stock.XCHNG (Bella)
88: Peasley, Sue (Winston)
89: Nasta, Sarah (Abby)
90: Smith, Michael (Captain Jack Sparrow)
91: Marchese, Melissa (Bijou)
92: Estes, Michelle (Samantha)
93: Pring, John/Stock.XCHNG (Seamus)
94: Flick, Marja/Stock.XCHNG (Zela)
95: Rosen-Zohar, Lily/Stock.XCHNG (Bella)
96: Mills, Pamela (Austin)
97: Schultz, Ronnie (Tessy May)
98: Dickinson, Robert (Bradley)
99: Duthie, Ken and Maria (Flip)
100: Davis, Keith (Rebo)
101: Schultz, Ronnie (Tessy May)
102: Hayes, Thomas (Mina)
103: Martin, Mindy (Frankie)
104: Beres, Igor/Stock.XCHNG (Master Blaster)
105: Bogues, Keith and Nancy (Scully)
106: Chafitz, Jeffrey (Burmey)
107: Duthie, Ken and Maria (Flip)
108: Schultz, Ronnie
109: Shpuntoff, Steven (Bailey the dog, Diablo the cat)
110: Jacobson, Rachel (Sammy)
111: Bogues, Keith and Nancy (Scully, Stryder)
112: Dwyer, Kevin and Jessica (Lukin)
113: Zampieri, Fabrizzio/Stock.XCHNG (Kebeck)
114: McCullough, Matt and Kate (Lola)

115: Schultz, Ronnie (Hunny)
116: Beineke, Deanna (Blackie)
117: Sorg, Aaron (Tyler)
118: Kasch, Allison (Maya)
119: Poe, Andrea (Sherman "Tank" Poe)
120: Terhune, Becky (Vinnie)
121: Bean, Brittany (Holly)
122: Bruess, Dan (Wiley)
123: Cain, Christy (Tucker)
124: Tverskaya, Ilona (Tiny)
125: Meuller, Jan (Missy)
126: Maxwell, Jane (Reverence, also known as Kookamonga)
127: Cartabio, Emilio (Sir Chadwick Diamond Star)
128: Anthony, Kim (Otis)
129: Rio, Boris/Stock.XCHNG (Oliver)
130: Maher, Alex/Stock.XCHNG (Nanook)
131: Rodda, Carol (Bella)
132: Richards, Barb (Hershey)
133: Terhune, Becky (Vinnie)
134: Clark III, James (Sir Taz Clark)
135: Densford, David (Brodie)
136: Weber, Elaine (Nikki)
137: Riley, Frank (Benji, Madison)
138: Schultz, Ronnie (Harry)
139: Dziedziech, Jennifer (Xena)
140: O'Nan-Johnson, Lucy (Murphy, Tucker)
141: Stanford, Renee (Maxy)
142: Clark III, James (Sir Taz Clark)
143: Jacobson, Rachel (Sammy)
144: Idem, Boni/Stock.XCHNG (Carlos)
145: Riggio, Steve (Molly)
146: Gainer, Jill (Sophie)
148: Rosen-Zohar, Lily/Stock.XCHNG (Bella the dog, Shimi the cat)
149: Mifsud, Therese (Jack)
150: Miata, Megan (Layla)
151: Noble, John/Stock.XCHNG (Bonny)
152: Een, Melanie (Rusty)
153: Krieb, Martha (Levi)
154: Dziedziech, Jennifer (Xena)
155: Clancy, Lori (Mia)
156: Noble, John/Stock.XCHNG (Bonny)
157: Schultz, Ronnie
158: Zayats, Yelena (Franky)
159: Poe, Andrea (Sherman "Tank" Poe)
160: Gainer, Jill (Sophie)
161: Cain, Christy (Tucker)
162: Schultz, Ronnie (Lily Rose)
163: Mammano, Angela (Lou)
164: Fiore, Jana (Lucy)
165: Clark III, James (Sir Taz Clark)
166: Dodson, Megan/Stock.XCHNG (Captain)
168: Zeno, Allison (Gotti Giovanni Zeno)
169: Mifsud, Therese (Jack the dog, Chica the bird)
170: Isaacson, Rob (Sunny, Chloe)
171: Tomcsak, Csaba/Stock.XCHNG (Lily)
172: Heath, Michelle (Angel)

173: Wilson, Melissa (Georgia)
174: McGoey, Teresa (Tucker, Diesel)
175: Dwyer, Kevin and Jessica (Dharma)
176: DiNucci, Lori Ann (Misty)
177: Evans, Shenandoah (Manhattan, also known as Manny)
178: Veltrie Family (Gus)
179: Thomas Photographic (Pugsley)
180: Nelson-Strumpf, Noah (Leo)
181: Dwyer, Kevin and Jessica (Tinkerbell)
182: Mosby, Tara (Mercedes)
183: Schultz, Ronnie (Lily Rose)
184: © Daniel Rutkowski 2005 (Lulu)
185: Dwyer, Kevin and Jessica (Dharma)
186: Gershman, Elizabeth (Orion)
187: Vaughan, Andy (remoH)
188: Krause, Anja (Sparky)
189: Wellstein, Bridgette (Marshall)
190: Margetts, Michelle (Chloe)
191: Thomas Photographic (Pugsley)
192: Dodson, Megan/Stock.XCHNG (Captain)
193: Weber, Elaine (Nikki)
194: Reid, Cindy (Quincy)
195: Jones, Jessica (Brandy Girl)
196: Schultz, Ronnie (Kai)
197: Ziegelbauer, Lynne (Tres, Dobbs)
198: Sandin, Patty (Spencer)
199: Comento, Lisa (Indy)
200: Rosen-Zohar, Lily/Stock.XCHNG (Bella the dog, Shimi the cat)
202: Broome, Chris (Kippa, Franklin, Moses, Jake)
203: Schultz, Ronnie
204: Kapitov, Irina (Coco Chanel)
205: McCullough, Matt and Kate (Poppy)
206: Classens, Adri/Stock.XCHNG (Kimba)
207: Rouda, Jean (Charlie, Romeo, Sandy)
208: Tice, Laura (Shorty, Daisy Duke)
209: Peasley, Sue (Winston)
210: Gordon, Reggie (Oreo)
211: Strom, Rita (Onyx, Shelly)
212: Rosen-Zohar, Lily/Stock.XCHNG (Bella the dog, Shimi the cat)
213: Dusenberry, Kathy (Odie, Izabella)
214: Een, Melanie (Rusty)
215: Heun, Christine (Tallulah Doghead)
216: Viola, Stephanie (Molly Mae Bean)
217: Reixach, Vicki/Stock.XCHNG (Boss the dog, Ona the cat)